Bannockburn, 1314:
The Bruce Triumphant

Bruce reviewing troops before the Battle of Bannockburn.

Bannockburn, 1314:
The Bruce Triumphant

Bannockburn
John E. Morris

The Battle of Bannockburn
Robert White

LEONAUR

Bannockburn, 1314: The Bruce Triumphant
Bannockburn
by John E. Morris
and
The Battle of Bannockburn
by Robert White

First published under the titles
Bannockburn
and
The Battle of Bannockburn

FIRST EDITION

Leonaur is an imprint
of Oakpast Ltd

ISBN: 978-1-78282-233-2 (hardcover)
ISBN: 978-1-78282-234-9(softcover)

http://www.leonaur.com

Contents

Bannockburn

Contents

CHAPTER 1

Thoughts on Bannockburn

The 600th anniversary of Bannockburn is an event that ought to make people think. Scotsmen are jubilant, and rightly so; Englishmen would do well to be thoughtful, and as, although medieval conditions do not exist today, human nature is much the same at all periods, certain reflections do not come amiss. One result of the study of old quarrels is the acknowledgement that war has had a greater influence than the school of J. R. Green, the scorner of the drum-and-trumpet theory of history, would allow. It has influenced constitutional progress. Of course Green himself knew this. All his admirers know the passage which couples Château Gaillard with Runnymede; the fall of the great Norman Castle and the subsequent loss of Normandy to the French made Magna Carta possible. Just in the same way the wars of Wallace and Bruce brought to a head the ceaseless contest between the English Crown and the Baronage, and made Magna Carta effectual.

From the purely military point of view England was passing through a crisis under the three Edwards. The development of longbow archery, which proved the value of the peasant in war, can be traced from Wales and the Welsh wars, through the Wallace and Bruce period, down to the day of Crécy. War in itself is revolting; yet it is impossible not to admire the combination of coolness and skill which makes for victory. More than that; war brings out a nation's resources and moulds national character. Thus a few minutes of reflection on an old battle will at least suggest the old and ever-needed lesson of readiness, of modesty, of profiting by mistakes, and of unanimity and a complete absence of class hatreds, if a nation is to be successful.

Bannockburn cannot be studied by itself. It is one event in a series. The most important it may be, yet one to be studied in the light of what came both before and after. It shows the evolution of the peasant to be as good a fighting man as the lord, but only on the condition that he is well led. The foot spearman triumphed over the mounted knight in all his pride; the man who kept his place in the ranks triumphed over the man who rode jealous of his neighbour; the nation whose king was supported both by nobles and by peasants triumphed over the nation whose nobles scorned alike their king, the peasant archers of their own army, and the peasant spearmen opposed to them. Bruce won independence for Scotland; he also taught the English to abate their pride and to combine, noble with archer, in future wars, or rather to re-learn a previous lesson of combination, which the English barons in their pride and factious opposition to their king had put aside.

The history of Bannockburn, when taken with the history of the wars before and after, helps us to understand the Anglo-Saxon character. The man of restless energy, who loves adventure for itself, who fights because fighting gives him something to do and enables him to show his masterfulness, who thinks that none but he has the right to fight, who if he is not fighting is engaged in a constitutional struggle against his king—which indeed is partly a class trouble and partly personal to himself, for the barons by no means always pulled together—who, at intervals when nothing else is stirring, crusades in Palestine or Africa or Prussia, who in fact must always be up and doing, is the Norman baron. The Anglo-Saxon is the stay-at-home. His ancestors indeed had come as pirates and conquerors, but the next generations settled down on the land; the pirates turned farmers, forgot how to fight, cowered before the Danes, rallied when well led and inspired by Alfred and Edward the Elder and their successors, collapsed once more when even the House of Alfred produced an Ethelred, were unable to rally to any purpose under Edmund Ironsides, and so let their country fall at one blow before William.

They let the burden of fighting be borne by the House of Godwin and a few energetic thegns and a professional bodyguard of housecarles. When once Hastings was fought and won and the few fighting men were dead, partly because Wessex and Mercia, East Anglia and Northumbria, could not combine for lack of leadership and a common bond of union, mostly because the churls and boors were rooted to the soil as peaceful farmers, they received new masters and sank to be villeins or semi-serfs. Spasmodically they showed some spirit. Rufus called some of them out. Henry I carried over some of them to

Normandy, and with their help beat Robert. The men of the North rose at the call of the Church, and beat back the Scots at the Battle of the Standard, Henry II saw their value, and by his assize of arms reorganised the old Anglo-Saxon fyrd or militia.

But a militia has inherent defects, for it cannot be trained systematically, and if it is called out for any length of time farming suffers, so that, although spasmodically a militia force may be raised to a certain degree of excellence, the system as a system is a bad one. Now the Norman barons were restive under the Williams and Henries because, having come to England as adventurers and having received lands in a conquered country, they resented the strong control of the Crown, the royal insistence upon strict payment of feudal dues, and the power of the Royal Court over their Manor Courts. Each wanted to be a little king over his own estates. Therefore their ideal was individualism. But the strong rule of Henry II created an official class which enabled the Crown to prevail against them. Of course with the reign of King John the problem was changed. Normandy was lost, and every baron had to decide whether he should be henceforward an Englishman or a Norman.

All those who preferred the island kingdom to the duchy were now, however pure might be their Norman blood, English barons, and they tended more and more to unite as a class against the Crown until they extorted from John their class liberties. Their strongest stand they made on the question of feudal service. William the Conqueror had granted lands to their ancestors on condition that they should fight for him without pay; but he was then both King of England and Duke of Normandy, whereas John was only king—the Duchy of Aquitaine does not count, for Henry II was the first to hold it, whereas feudal service had been instituted by William I. Therefore the cry of "No feudal service across the sea" directly preceded the demand for the Great Charter.

Of course their object in extorting the Great Charter was to win their own liberties, not the freedom of all classes of unborn Englishmen for generations to come; not the control of all taxation by the Commons, which did not yet exist, but their special right not to have to pay aids and scutages without their own consent. An "aid" was a money grant upon a special occasion; "scutage" was money paid in lieu of feudal service; and both were in proportion to the number of knights that each baron, or indeed even quite humble men who held land directly from the Crown, owed for war. Therefore the military consequence of the Great Charter was that the king could not declare war or enforce feudal service or collect a scutage without consent. If he fought on his own initiative he must do it at his own cost. Both for men and for money for a serious undertaking he was dependent upon his barons. "Men" here means mounted men exclusively; the feudal system provided the king with heavy cavalry only.

To understand the Norman spirit we have to look at one special district—the Marches of Wales. For a period of about two centuries the Norman lords were able to show their love of adventure in this particular district where there was no restraint upon them. The Crown, partly it would seem to give to the barons just that something to do for which their souls yearned and therefore to divert their attention from England, and partly to reduce the breezy and freedom-loving Welsh by a cheap method, allowed certain lords to wage war and to conquer on their own behalf as much of Wales as they could.

As a matter of fact the Earls of Chester conquered but very little of North Wales; and the Mortimers conquered some, but not very much, of mid-Wales; but in the century between William I and Henry II most of South Wales was won. There the March estates were created; there were erected the castles, first the moated earthen mounds, which were crowned with wooden stockades and towers, and later the stone keeps, which are the outward and visible signs of the earlier and the later Norman periods. The Welsh offered a keen resistance, particularly in the Valley of the Usk, the land of Gwent. But, when at last overcome, they fought under their Norman lords against other Welsh. They followed Strongbow and his brother raiders to Ireland, and in battle the native Irish and the Irish Danes went down before the combination of mailed Norman horse and South Wales archers.

For this is the main fact; the land where the true long-bow was first effectively used was South Wales. It was a bow of wild elm, ugly, unpolished, rough, but stiff and strong; so says the native historian of Wales, Gerald de Barry, and the conclusion to which he comes is that in the field mounted men and archers should always be combined. The whole of Strongbow's army of invasion was something short of 400 horse and 2000 archers. It was a Norman-Welsh, far indeed from being an English, invasion of Ireland.

We do not possess about any army of Richard I such definite information as the actual pay-rolls give us for Edward I. We simply know that the Anglo-Norman contingent at Acre and Arsuf was but a fraction of the crusading host. We can guess that it was mostly Norman;

how many or how few were the Saxons in the retinues of Richard himself and his barons we cannot determine, but that they were quite few is practically certain. That all Crusaders knew the value of good archers, whether mounted or on foot, to combat the Turkish horse archers is clear. The tactics in the East consisted of putting a screen of foot, mostly bow-armed, to shield the horses of the mailed men against the arrows of the Turks, and of then giving the word for the horsemen to charge through the screen at the right moment. This was done by Philip of France at Acre before Richard's arrival, as well as by Richard himself at Arsuf.

But the typical bow-men of a crusading army were crossbow-men, Genoese and Pisans, and it was the cross-bow that had the best repute. Richard himself was alive to the value of the long-bow and tried to obtain South Welsh archers, but they were doubtless few in numbers and not anxious to enlist for distant service in Palestine or France. For this fact is prominent, and it is entirely germane to our purpose, that in Western Europe infantry were of no account in spite of the experience of the Crusades. For instance, at the Battle of Bouvines in 1214 a mass of foot was pushed forward in front of the mailed cavalry, but was entirely useless in the battle and may be said to have been merely exposed to be slaughtered. In England the cross-bow was valued and considered to be the best missile weapon down to the reign of Edward I, but the crossbow-men were quite few in numbers, and those few were chiefly professional mercenaries. Some indeed were Londoners, but most were Netherlanders or Gascons and, as mercenaries, they came under the ban of the Great Charter.

As a critical period, both from the constitutional and from the military point of view, let us take the days of Simon de Montfort. Constitutionally the barons of his period appeared to be contending for their class privileges against the Crown so as to make the Great Charter effectual. But it is well known that by no means all the barons were Montfortians. The personal element came in, as it always must come in. Take Gilbert of Clare, Earl of Gloucester, who fought side by side with Simon at Lewes and against Simon at Evesham. Why was this? Chiefly it was because Llewelyn of Wales was Simon's ally, for, as the result of the whole baronial struggle of the reigns of John and Henry III, the Welsh had been gaining ground as against the Lords Marchers.

As Lord of Glamorgan, Gloucester was one of the chief Marchers. He was keen enough to stand up as Earl against King in England, but he was not going to allow Llewelyn to grow to such strength as to weaken him as Lord Marcher; Llewelyn being Simon's ally, Glamorgan was in danger. Also, from the military point of view, the actions at Lewes and Evesham are of interest because the barons and the mounted men alone were deemed to be of any value. As we saw just now, the lesson of the Crusades had been thrown away and the barons wished to keep to themselves the fighting, even as they put themselves and their own liberties forward against the king. That is to say, they themselves wished alone to be in evidence, whether they were fighting or whether they were agitating against the Crown.

Any keen lover of history is quick to resent a charge of pedantry, and such a charge may often be made in connection with the exact use of words. But every man must use words according to the meanings that they bear to him and the ideas that they suggest to him. Green and Freeman were right from their own standpoint when they called the Angles and Saxons, even as they called themselves, English. They implied that our nation is still English in the same sense, having absorbed into itself Danes and Normans.

To others, however, it appears that the English nation in history and today has both Saxon characteristics and Danish and Norman characteristics, and that the Saxons did not absorb but were leavened by the Normans. Consequently we should call the old race Saxon or Anglo-Saxon, the mixed race English. We have a very definite date at which we can first use the word "English" in such a sense, *viz.* 1204, the date of John's loss of Normandy. Then the Montfortian period, being as it were the outcome of the struggle for the Charter, was a time when the barons were vitally conscious of their position as Englishmen. They protested against the King's foreign ministers and favourites as if their own ancestors had never been foreigners, and Simon de Montfort himself lost his authority amongst them because, though he posed as the anti-foreigner, he was himself not purely English by blood.

We can continue this thought now into the reign of Edward I. The wars against the Welsh and the Scots, long before the Hundred Years War began in France, cannot but have given a stronger idea of English nationality. A baron cannot fight in Wales or in Scotland without feeling himself to be an Englishman, however pure his Norman blood may still be. But we have to make a strong distinction between the Welsh and the Scottish campaigns. In Wales all the barons of Edward I served as a feudal duty, but their hearts were not in a war in

Scotland. The reason is that as Lords Marchers they were determined to support their king in crushing Llewelyn and the still independent section of the Welsh. Almost every magnate was likewise a Lord Marcher. Not only was Gloucester Lord of Glamorgan; Humphrey Bohun, hereditary Constable and Earl of Hereford, was Lord of Brecknock; Roger Bigod, hereditary Marshal and Earl of Norfolk, was Lord of Chepstow; the king's own brother, Edmund of Lancaster, was Lord of Monmouth; the Earl of Lincoln in the course of the last war against Llewelyn received the marcher lordship of Denbigh; Roger Mortimer had great estates in Shropshire and Herefordshire, and likewise in mid-Wales.

And so all the lords, whether great or small, whether Montfortians or Royalists in the last reign, followed Edward I against Llewelyn as a matter of course. In 1277 they served for five months; in 1282-3 for 15 months; and then again on the rising of Rhys in 1287, and of Madoc in 1294-5. Each seemed to consider it to be a point of honour to serve unpaid, for thus the Crown was under an obligation to him, and he was defending his own march lands as well as fighting for the King of England. It is important to insist upon this point because, if these men served the Crown as a feudal duty, they were likewise intensely keen to maintain their privileges as free and almost independent princes on the marches of Wales. When Edward I made a royal progress through Wales after the conquest of 1283, Gloucester received and entertained him in Glamorgan as if he were a brother monarch rather than a subject.

Edward I distinctly wished to suppress the customs of the marches, and in particular the right claimed by all the marcher lords to wage private war at their own will. In course of time Gloucester gave him the opportunity that he sought, for he continually raided Hereford's lands in Brecknock. The king was very patient and tried to bring the earl to reason, even giving to him his own daughter in marriage, but Gloucester was proud and defiantly waged his private war. The scene of battle was a strip of debatable land lying up in the mountains between the Clare march of Glamorgan and the Bohun march of Brecknock. Edward at last asserted himself, and ordered both earls to appear to answer for their conduct.

Hereford appeared before the Royal Judges, but Gloucester refused. The judges on the king's order tried to empanel a jury of the other marcher lords so as to secure through them a verdict condemning the greatest marcher lords. They refused to sit as a jury or to swear on the Book. It was, they said, against the use and custom of the marchers. The judges answered that by his prerogative the king was above both use and custom, but the lords prevailed and a jury of men of lower station had to be empanelled. The facts were proved and a verdict returned against Gloucester. Then Edward went in person to Wales and held his court at Abergavenny. Gloucester, at last cowed, now put in an appearance. Sentence was finally pronounced against him at Westminster:

> Because the earls had dared to do by their own liberty of the march violent deeds which would have met with condign punishment elsewhere outside the marches.

They were committed to prison and their lands confiscated for life. As a matter of fact they were soon allowed to redeem their bodies by payment of fines, Gloucester of 10,000 *marks*, Hereford of 1000, and their lands were restored to them.

Two points are clear. Firstly, Gloucester was the chief offender in waging this private war, but Hereford, who had only been on the defensive originally, was also imprisoned and fined. And, secondly, the whole body of lords marchers evidently resented the royal interference as a blow against the independence of them all. They valued march privilege because only in this corner of the country could they claim to be free from royal restrictions.

Gloucester died a sadder and a wiser man, leaving by his royal wife three daughters and a son, who was killed at Bannockburn. Hereford lived nursing a sense of injury, and in alliance with Norfolk defied Edward in 1297 and 1298. And indeed Edward had made a mistake by bringing down his mailed fist too strongly, for he had offended a class and had been over-severe on one particular earl of that class.

In the last Welsh war of 1295 Edward offended Norfolk and deposed him for a time from the marshalship; he then gave a formal written promise that when he ordered his marshal to serve in a different region of Wales away from his royal person it was not to be taken as a precedent. Evidently Norfolk was now on the look-out for some opportunity to defy the masterful king when law and custom were on his side. Let us remember that in this very year 1295 Edward summoned his model Parliament. Faced by war in Wales, war in Scotland, and war from France, he wished to confer with Parliament that "what concerned all should be approved by all, and common dangers should be met in common," and Parliament voted to him liberal supplies.

Victorious over the Welsh in 1295, Edward beat Balliol at Dunbar in 1296, annexed Scotland as he thought was his right as Balliol's overlord, and garrisoned the castles. Next he turned his attention to the French war. And then the storm broke over his head. The story is well known, but it is not out of place to give the facts here so that the clerical and baronial opposition may be put clearly in relation to events in Scotland. Our main authority for the details is Walter of Hemingburgh, but the dates and the wording of various royal writs of summons must be carefully considered, for here, if at no other period in English history, foreign war and civil strife must be studied together.

Parliament met at Bury St Edmunds on November 3, 1296, then in London on January 14, 1297; a tax of one-twelfth on property was demanded from the people, one-eighth from towns, one-fifth from the clergy. Robert of Winchelsea, Archbishop of Canterbury, relying on a papal bull, refused to allow the clergy to pay. Edward promptly outlawed the clergy. The Archbishop-elect of York, and several bishops and others, gave way and put the fifth where the royal servants could find it; the lands of Canterbury were seized. Next Edward seized the wool and hides of the export-merchants, and requisitioned vast supplies of com and meat; he had the right to a "custom" on wool and the right of "pre-emption" on victuals, and he gave receipts for what he took; but he went beyond bounds. *Et multae fiebant oppressiones in populo terrae.* Here was the opportunity of the earls.

At Salisbury, February 24, in a "parliament without the clergy," the magnates refused to serve oversea, evidently basing their refusal on the historic opposition to John. Hereford the Constable and Norfolk the Marshal were the leaders, and their private reasons for revenge on the king, discussed just now, could be satisfied at last. The professed law-loving king had put himself in the wrong. He might threaten that they should go or hang, but the marshal could retort with right on his side *"Nec ibo nee pendebo,"* for feudal service outside the island could not be exacted. Supported by many barons, they armed and turned away from their lands the tax-collectors. Then they demanded that he should "confirm the Charters."

Edward, it seems clear from the facts of his wars, preferred paid service to feudal; if he could raise enough money by parliamentary grants, he was much more free to act and to command obedience on the field; the earls preferred to do feudal service, because thus they put him under an obligation to them for a war in Wales or Scotland. But by insisting that they could not be compelled on their feudal tenure to cross the sea they seemed to extort from him the very thing that he really preferred, namely payment for service. As regards the wool and victuals, he distinctly promised repayment to the last farthing, and excused himself "as he was acting in the cause of the people rather than of himself as their protector and defender." A national war against France should be supported by the nation, and the king's prerogative alone could secure national unity.

Reconciled temporarily to the archbishop, leaving him and the veteran soldier Reginald Grey as guardians to Prince Edward, refusing to confirm the Charters immediately as he had not then his full council with him, and calling on the two earls not to do any harm to the country in his absence, Edward sailed on August 22 for Flanders. He already knew of Wallace's rising, but the Confirmation of the Charters was the great question at stake, and he had no fears about Scotland. Norfolk and Hereford and their party were in arms. Grey and the Prince's council issued various writs to men to come armed to Rochester on September 8, ostensibly to discuss measures for the defence of the coast; Norfolk and Hereford and others were summoned to London on September 30; two knights from each shire were to come to London on October 6 to receive their copies of the Confirmation of the Charters; then three loyal earls, several barons and knights who had served Edward in Wales and Scotland, sheriffs of counties and arrayers of troops, were to bring knights and servientes to London on October 6 at the royal wages.

Two facts stand out here; it was evidently intended that the confirmation should be granted, and the loyalists were to be armed as against Norfolk and Hereford. But on September 11 fell a bolt from the blue, for Wallace, known already to be in arms but despised as a beggarly outlaw, destroyed at Stirling Bridge a body of English horse. It was not a battle on a great scale; with the king in Flanders, and both rebel and loyal barons arming in anticipation of a stormy Parliament a month hence, there cannot have been a very large number of English soldiers in Scotland. But the result was as tremendous as if thousands had fought on either side. Panic fell upon the English garrisons in Scotland, and castles were deserted. Wallace raided Cumberland and Northumberland. It was not the time for an armed dispute at home. Prince Edward issued the confirmation on October 10. The loyal barons swore on the gospels that they would hold Norfolk and Hereford guiltless towards the king. Troops, raised apparently to fight Norfolk and Hereford if the need should arise, were ordered northwards.

All the circumstances tend to show that the defeat at Stirling saved England, if not from certain civil war, at least from the imminent danger of civil war. King Edward accepted the position, and confirmed the charters in Flanders. A force of both loyalists and recalcitrant lords went up north for a winter campaign, and saved Roxburgh and Berwick.

Returning to England in March, 1298, Edward was collecting a new army. But a further difficulty arose. His son had confirmed in England, and he had confirmed in Flanders. Norfolk and Hereford now demanded that he should confirm again, himself and in England. He positively refused; this was equivalent to doubting his royal word. Then they refused to march towards Scotland. There was a deadlock. At last Antony Bek, Bishop of Durham, and the loyal earls swore a personal oath that the king would abide by his word. The army marched, fought and beat Wallace at Falkirk, and—marched back again; ostensibly this was due to lack of victuals, really the recalcitrants, having made the king once sensible of their power, wished to press their advantage.

A Scottish war meant nothing to them; they had no marches on that border to defend against a Scottish Llewelyn; and having done their 40 days of feudal service they claimed that they were within their rights in going home. It cannot indeed be proved that they based their opposition on the 40 days' limit. The official excuse of lack of victuals is duly recorded by Hemingburgh. But we are fully justified in reading between the lines, especially as in the following years we find a 40 days' campaign quite common. Hereford died that winter, but Norfolk evidently had strong support, and Edward's wish to carry on the campaign through the winter, as he had twice done in Wales, was frustrated.

The year 1299 was blank as regards war. An effort to raise an army for the winter of 1299-1300 failed. Disaffection was in the air. The tenants of the Bishop of Durham declared that they were bound by their tenure only to serve at home in defence, not to invade Scotland; even the bishop himself, who tried to act as arbiter, at last declared that the two earls were originally right in their demand for the confirmation. The infantry levies of the Northern counties deserted. Edward now offered to confirm with the saving clause *salvo iure coronae*—i.e. "saving king's prerogative"—but was finally forced to confirm unconditionally without the clause. Evidently, even then, he could only raise an army for 1300 by strict feudal summons; his opponents found it their best weapon against them that he should need their unpaid feudal services; and that year saw merely a campaign of 40 days and the fall of one castle. In 1301 in a Parliament at Lincoln he confirmed again fully and unconditionally, and in 1301 there was a paltry campaign of two months, but no formal feudal muster.

But the tide at last turned. The pope claimed Scotland as a fief of the Papal See, and Archbishop Winchelsea pressed the claim. The barons then joined their king, for they resented such outside interference. Perhaps a great many had opposed Edward as they had seen the success of Norfolk's and Hereford's first opposition, and by a reaction were satisfied as he had given way. At least now the two chief leaders were losing their influence. The archbishop was exiled. Norfolk was stripped of lands, earldom, marshalship, and received them back for life only; the official excuse that he made a voluntary surrender in order to spite his brother who was his heir is, to use modern slang, a little too thin, and the obvious fact is that Edward, having got Norfolk in his power now that the other barons were satisfied by the unconditional confirmation, seized his opportunity and stripped him to the skin.

Then Edward called a formal feudal muster for 1303, remained in Scotland continuously through the winter in face of all difficulties, recaptured Stirling Castle by means of a powerful artillery in 1304, and seemed at last to be victorious. But the spirit of the Scots, roused by Wallace in 1297, had not been extinguished, and from Edward's point of view baronial factiousness had wasted six years and allowed that spirit to get strong. When Bruce, having time after time sworn fealty to Edward, killed Red Comyn and elected finally to be king and patriot, the chance of crushing Scotland was gone. Edward I died on his way up to Scotland in 1307.

The connection between Bannockburn and the ordinances must be studied as closely as that between Wallace's rising and the confirmation. Bishop Stubbs has pointed out to us how the aims of the united barons who won the Great Charter from John were no longer the aims of Norfolk and Hereford in 1297, or of the Lords Ordainers in 1310 onwards. Personal ambition, a love of thwarting the Crown when Scottish affairs gave them their chance, an open desire to get the control of England into the hands of a small party, are too apparent. Edward II meant to crush opposition with a high hand, even as his father at last, though only at the cost of unconditional surrender on the main question of the Confirmation, had crushed Norfolk and

Winchelsea. But we know that he had not his father's high ideas, and he had Piers Gaveston as his favourite, the Gascon upstart who jeered at the earls and found nicknames for them. So between 1307 and 1310 nothing was done, and Bruce grew in strength. In March, 1310, the Lords Ordainers were acknowledged formally by Edward as a Committee of Control, so to speak, and in August they drew up certain ordinances; the archbishop pronounced excommunication against all who should violate them.

In expectation that his submission would induce the barons to support him in Scotland, Edward in June summoned a feudal muster, and in August sent a second summons; the rendezvous was to be at Berwick on September 8th. But a very poor muster it was. Hereford, son of Edward I's old enemy, and hereditary constable by right, failed to appear, and on September 19th merely ten men-at-arms were registered as his feudal contingent. Thomas of Lancaster, the king's cousin and son of Edmund of Lancaster who had always been loyal to Edward I, and Guy, Earl of Warwick, and many others, sent similarly each a bare minimum of soldiers. The feudal host came in by driblets, and in the whole month of September only 500 men were registered, and of these only 37 were knights. Twenty men came as late as October. A feeble inroad of barely 40 days was the result.

We pass on to the acceptance by Edward of the ordinances, the exile, the return, the surrender, and the execution, in violation of faith, of Piers Gaveston. The selfishness and perfidy of the Lords Ordainers were too bad even for those days. Gloucester, son of Edward I's enemy and Edward I's daughter, was converted to loyalty. So was Aymer of Valence, Earl of Pembroke, grandson of King John's widow, for he was especially offended in that Piers had surrendered to him originally. Even Hereford was touched. But Lancaster and Warwick were grimly satisfied with what they had done. In 1313 there was a hollow reconciliation, and Lancaster and Warwick were formally pardoned by the king. But in the meanwhile castle after castle in Scotland had fallen to Bruce. Stirling in 1314 was in danger, and was to be surrendered unless rescued before the end of June. Edward had quite enough spirit for war, and hoped that the reaction against the earls after the murder of Piers was strong enough to justify him. So, without the consent of his barons in Parliament, he summoned a feudal muster. Says a contemporary chronicler, who wrote the *Vita Edwardi Secundi:*

The king ordered his barons and earls to come to his help. The earls answered that it would be better for all to come to a Parliament, for the ordinances demanded it. He said the matter was urgent, and he could not wait for a Parliament. They refused to come that they might not offend against the ordinances. But his private advisers counselled him to summon the feudal retinues and proceed boldly to Scotland. What about the Earl of Gloucester? they said, what about Pembroke and Hereford, Robert Clifford Hugh Despenser, and the royal household and other barons? All these will come with their soldiers, and there is no need to be anxious about the other earls.

And a later chronicler. Abbot Burton of Meaux, reviewing the defeat of Bannockburn says:

The misfortune of the defeat was imputed, not so much to the presumption and pride of the English, as to the excommunication to which they made themselves liable by going against the ordinances. That this is true is wonderfully confirmed by the coincidence that none of the Lords Ordainers who fought in the battle escaped capture or death, except Pembroke, who fled unarmed.

And so we come to a final conclusion; as long as king and barons were violently opposed to each other there was no chance of a successful war in Scotland. Bruce alone profited by the ordinances.

CHAPTER 2

A Typical Edwardian Army

The question before us is, was the English Army at Bannockburn 100,000 strong? First we have to consider that the chroniclers of the period were all clerics, except indeed Gray of Heton who was a soldier and therefore our prime authority. Chroniclers did not understand numbers; 10,000 or 100,000 meant nothing to them. Partly they loved to exaggerate, and partly also a sort of inborn love of blood and slaughter must have influenced them and their readers, just as today an evening edition sells best when it can advertise a very large loss of life. Another consideration is that the old chroniclers, and modern historians also, have been misled by the need of multiplying figures, whether those of the Bannockburn campaign, or those of Crécy; and indeed in all wars, such as the ancient Persian Wars as described by Herodotus, we find the same problem.

The historian has certain figures, right or wrong—usually wrong,— and on his own authority doubles or trebles or quadruples because he thinks that for every soldier there must be a certain proportion of inferior soldiers or camp-followers. A great many of Froissart's errors can be rectified in this way. Let us say that he is told there were 1000 knights in an army; he promptly multiplies by four or five to include the inferior mounted men. If he had been told that there were 200 knights and that he must multiply by five to give a total of 1000, he would have been right. It will be seen that this argument is of very great importance when we come to consider the details of the feudal system. Modern historians sometimes fall into this error with their eyes open, accepting unscientifically the old untrustworthy figures for the Bannockburn campaign, and it is probable that national patriotism has had its share in making the 100,000 to be generally accepted.

The last chapter showed us the importance and pride of the bar-

Ben Ledi   Gillies Hill

PANORAMIC VIEW OF THE REPUTED SITE OF THE BATTLE

THE SUGGESTED SITE IS SEEN BEHI

Stirling Castle   St Ninian's   The Abbey Craig
Coxet Hill   The Borestone

...NNOCKBURN TAKEN FROM ABOVE FOOT O' GREEN FARM.
.. NINIANS'S AND THE BORESTONE

ons. Therefore if we are to consider any typical Edwardian army we must take the barons first. In the Montfortian War, both at Lewes and Evesham, they alone were in evidence with their mounted retinues. In his Welsh wars, in the two pitched battles at Builth and Maesmadoc, and then again in the Scottish campaign at Falkirk, Edward I and his officers knew well the need of combination of horse with foot. But in all those three battles the horsemen began the attack without the foot, and it was not until the foot had been brought up that the victory was gained.

The evidence is to be found in certain documents. For some years we possess the Marshals' Registers on which were enrolled the exact numbers of all the feudal contingents brought to the king's standard, together with the men's names. For several campaigns we also possess the pay-rolls, which give us the exact numbers of the horse or foot engaged. But the series of the pay-rolls is by no means complete, and frequently in some critical year we are deprived of their assistance. Another class of documents is the series of horse-lists on which were enrolled the name of every horseman in the king's pay, together with the value and colour and points of his horse, so that if the animal was killed on the king's service the value could be made good to the owner. When we possess a horse-list we have first-class evidence of some campaign which cannot be controverted.

Lastly upon certain rolls called the *Rotuli Scotiae* are entered the official duplicates of every writ connected with Scotland sent out by the king in some particular year; and amongst other entries we are told that such and such a baron or one of his followers has the king's "protection," that is to say, a sort of passport declaring that he was under the king's protection during the campaign and therefore anybody who did harm to the man's property in England would offend the king.

Of course one cannot imagine that every single mounted soldier in a campaign had such protection, but we do gain in this way the names of at least a large proportion of those who were serving. Now for the year 1314 almost every document has disappeared. We have no marshals' register because it was not a strictly feudal campaign; we have no pay-roll and no horse-list. But we have the Scottish Roll of the year, and by it we know that at least 830 earls and barons of high degree and retainers were on their way to Scotland, even if they did not all actually reach the field of Bannockburn.

Here must be added that the father of all genuine original work on this period of Scottish history is Mr Joseph Bain, who edited in four volumes the *Calendar of Documents relating to Scotland.*

A. FEUDAL CAVALRY

William the Conqueror, after the Battle of Hastings, allotted the confiscated estates of the Saxons to his Norman and French followers on condition that they provided him with soldiers for his wars. This is "knight service." Imagination likes to depict 60,000, or at least 32,000, as the "gross total of the full number of horsemen which the Conqueror could demand from the full body of his tenants-in-chief. Either figure is wildly absurd, and 6400 is nearer to the truth. As instances we may take Eustace, Count of Boulogne, whose feudal service was rated at 120 knights; William of Warrenne, Lord of the Rape of Lewes, at 60; the Lord of Odell (Wadehelle or Wahulle) at 30; the Abbot of Peterborough at 60; the Abbot of St Albans at six.

The king would only demand a period of 40 days of unpaid service, and from this it is clear that he had before his eyes the need of defending England from an attack of the Danes or of providing against an Anglo-Saxon rising; no war outside of England could possibly be settled in 40 days. It is well known that after his reign other Kings allowed money payment in lieu of feudal service, and this is known as scutage. Here we find our evidence. Henry II made enquiries of all the sheriffs, who were to ask the tenants-in-chief of their counties what were the numbers of men that their ancestors had owed to William I, and they made reply in what are called *Cartae Baronum*, the charters of the barons. The replies usually began:

I have always heard from my ancestors that so many knights were due to King William.

Then at the end of a feudal campaign the sheriff of each county drew up a list of the sums of money owed by way of scutage in case none of the tenants had served in the war and, if they had served, they had to prove it and so be quit of scutage. Therefore for the reigns of Henry III and Edward I we are very lucky in possessing scutage lists which tell us the exact number of knights owed in each county; they are to be found in the accounts of the sheriffs of the counties which were fastened together and rolled up in pipe rolls.

But in course of time this system of raising horsemen was changed, and one would say that either inability to acknowledge that the change was made, or perhaps downright ignorance, has contributed largely to continue the error of high numbers. Of course no war can possibly be finished in 40 days; therefore very naturally a king would say to his barons, "Bring fewer horsemen and serve longer." John and Henry III certainly did this, and the new system was in full working order when Edward I came to the throne. A baron was said to "recognise" some small number as his sufficient quota in place of the gross total.

Thus the Earl of Gloucester in place of 455 knights brought to Edward I's standard ten; the Earl of Hereford in place of 125 brought three; the Lord of Odell in place of 30 brought three; the Abbot of Peterborough's 60 was reduced to five, but the Abbot of St Albans, probably owing to the increase in wealth of his abbey since the Conquest, was still rated at six.

How the new numbers were fixed it is impossible to state. Probably each baron or cleric made his own bargain with the king, and the result is that we have now two separate sets of figures, the scutage lists in the pipe rolls based upon the old figures of William I, and the marshals' registers showing exactly how many horsemen in small quotas were brought in some particular feudal campaign.

Now we have to state very definitely that in the same interval the meaning of the word knight had changed. Under William I a "knight" or *miles* was the ordinary horseman of the period as we see him depicted in the Bayeux Tapestry. The evidence of Domesday Book is slight, for it was a register of the value of land for taxation, but occasionally the word *miles* is used, and we find that such a man was of quite an inferior position and by no means a knight of chivalry. But by the reign of Edward I "knight" or *miles* did mean the superior horseman of chivalry, who had been dubbed, who is called *chevalier* or *dominus* or "sir," and is of rank distinctly above the ordinary horseman. The word *serviens* or *scutiferus* or *constabularius* or *valettus* or *homo ad arma* is now given to the inferior horseman in the ranks.

Therefore if we compare Gloucester's figures in the two reigns, 455 would be the gross total of horsemen of all ranks owed to the king, but the ten knights actually brought to the king's standard were superior horsemen or *domini*, and the conclusion is that the 455 are not to be multiplied, but that the ten must be multiplied so as to give a proportion of inferior to superior horsemen. Perhaps we should not do wrong in multiplying by five. In that case Gloucester's contingent of ten knights represents a troop of 50 of all ranks, and the Lord of Odell's three would represent 12 to 15. Chroniclers accustomed to multiply would be very easily tempted to multiply William's figures also, and so our gross total of 6400 would be raised to 32,000, which is the actual figure given in Henry Ill's reign by an official of the Treasury, who ought to have known better.

The practical result of this change of system was that when Edward I went to war against Llewelyn in 1277 the marshal registered at headquarters a little over 200 knights, representing the feudal retinues of magnates, a few clerics, and several barons of medium standing. Many small tenants contributed one or two or three *servientes*, and two *servientes* might be sent to the army as the equivalent of one knight. It may be calculated that the full strength of heavy feudal cavalry in that campaign was about 1000 men. But it is quite clear that the magnates, as they are called, *i.e.* the earls and the greater barons, served for the whole campaign, and preferred to serve as a right or a feudal duty without pay. The medium and lesser barons might, and usually did, sandwich a period of 40 days without pay between two periods of pay.

Now, in the last chapter we saw that when matters were badly strained between Edward I and his barons their strongest weapon against the king was that they were not compelled to serve more than 40 days, and that they thus reduced war to a farce. In 1298, 1300, and 1301, there was a mere 40 days' campaign, and yet the barons had only brought to the king the reduced quota of men; that is to say, they brought a bare minimum of a retinue, and yet claimed that they need only fight for the 40 days.

If they could do this against Edward I, they naturally could put more pressure upon Edward II, and in 1310 not only was the campaign a paltry affair of 40 days, but also the feudal contingents were almost all sent in *servientes* only and not in knights; at Berwick that year 37 knights and 472 *servientes* were registered by the marshal, and here we cannot multiply. In fact there are three distinct steps; to a popular war against Llewelyn the lords bring a quota of knights, to whom must be added lesser horsemen, and serve for the whole campaign; to an unpopular war in Scotland, *tempore* Edward I, they bring similar quotas, but serve only for 40 days; to a war in Scotland, tempore Edward II, they do not bring, but merely send to represent them the lowest possible number of inferior horsemen. The legendary number of 60,000 of William the Conqueror turns out to be a great exaggeration for 6000 or a trifle more; practically a king may expect about 1000 horsemen at a feudal muster, but Edward II obtains 500 of the worst quality.

B. Paid Cavalry.

Obviously a system of pay was to the king's advantage. It gave promise of discipline and enabled him to brigade various units of horse into an organised body, whereas the individual feudal contingents, especially if they were small ones, would have had little power of combination. The normal rates of pay at the period were 4s. a day for an earl, or baron, or one of those professional captains who were the king's chief officers and are known as bannerets, 2s. for an ordinary knight, and is for an inferior horseman or *serviens*. These were the rates paid by the king, and the men or the captains of the contingents had to find their equipment and their food, so how much of the money finally descended to the men in the ranks cannot be calculated. Even earls, much as they wished to make the king dependent on them in war, were willing to take his pay for an extraordinary campaign, as in 1287 when Rhys ap Meredyth revolted in South Wales, and again in the winter of 1297-8 after Wallace's victory at Stirling Bridge.

The pay brought into most prominence the professional captain or banneret; it would be unfair to call him a mercenary. He might indeed be a tenant-in-chief of the king owing the service of a few knights. Such men served Edward I in war after war, were always in evidence as his chief arrayers of troops, and between wars frequently garrisoned his castles. They usually served the king under contract. We have a good instance when Aymer de Valence, titular Earl of Pembroke and the king's cousin, contracted with the king to keep on foot in time of peace a small number of men, and in war to bring him a squadron of 50; Thomas and Maurice of Berkeley sub-contracted with Aymer to bring most of the 50. These contracts are extant, and may be seen in Mr Bain's *Calendar*, vol. II; and there must have been many of the kind.

There were many landowners and men of substance in England who were not feudal tenants. These were by the Statute of Winchester compelled to have suitable arms and armour and horses ready at the king's call when he should need them, provided that they had property of £20 and over. Others whose property was £15 and over were expected to have inferior arms and horses. Besides this, Edward I compelled the men of the £20 class to take knighthood. The evidence that we have makes it an indubitable fact that such men were paid whenever they took the field. There was no effort on the part of any King of England to compel either the £20 or the £15 class to serve as a feudal duty. To the paid cavalry must next be added the king's household—knights and *servientes regis*—many of whom were foreigners, but in this period of history the employment of foreign mercenaries was not at all common.

Once in Wales Edward I had a corps of Gascons for a few months—210 horse and 1313 foot. In 1298 he had just over 100 Gascon horse. From time to time we find a handful of Germans in England, and in the early years of Edward III a few Hainaulters who came over in the train of John, uncle of Philippa of Hainault. One of them, Jehan le Bel, we may remark *en passant,* was afterwards the best chronicler of Edward Ill's wars. Just a few Irish were brought over, but at rare intervals; in 1296 Edward I had in his pay 310 men-at-arms, 266 light cavalry, 2570 foot, under the command of the Earl of Ulster and seven bannerets; and in 1301 264 men-at-arms, 391 light cavalry, 1580 foot. But ever since the days of the Great Charter Englishmen had viewed mercenaries with suspicion.

Now when we reckon together the feudal and the paid cavalry in particular campaigns we find that 1000 is the average figure in Edward I's Welsh wars, some 400 or 500 paid, and perhaps an equal number of feudal contingents continuing to serve after the 40 days were over. When he went to Flanders in 1297 and it was decided that all the troops were to be in his pay and none feudal, a horse-list gives us 800 as the exact figure. In the winter of 1297-8 while Edward I was still in Flanders, 750 cavalry were in pay on the border of Scotland against Wallace.

At the Battle of Falkirk in 1298 two horse-lists, one of the king's household and one of paid cavalry not in the household, give us a total of 1300; and the feudal contingents on that occasion may have been anything between 500 and 1000. We have no Marshal's Register for that year and there was no scutage taken for non-service, and therefore it was not a strictly feudal campaign; but the Scottish Roll of the year gives us a large number of names of men who were serving with the important earls and barons. A very generous calculation might put the total of the cavalry that year at 2400, but that is an extreme figure.

The horsemen of both grades, knights and *servientes* are to be reckoned as heavy cavalry. The armour of the period is well known to us from many a brass and other monumental evidence. Superior men wore mailed shirts and leggings, and a heavy helm which rested upon the shoulders. Small additional pieces of plate armour were just beginning to be fashionable, and these would have been strapped on to protect the vulnerable joints, such as the knee or shoulder or elbow. But it is highly probable that the inferior men substituted boiled leather in place of iron mail.

The horses were likewise armoured or, in medieval language, were *coöperti*, that is to say, "covered." They were big and heavy animals and cost anything between £5 and £100, money of that day, and as a rule it is considered that money of that day should be multiplied by 15 to give us modern prices. The great men often rode extremely valuable Spanish, or at least imported, *destriers* worth £50 or £100, and the troopers of their retinues mostly had rounseys—a term familiar to us from Chaucer—averaging about £10. The qualification of the man in the ranks who drew his shilling a day was that he rode a "covered" horse capable of carrying its armoured rider and its own horse-armour.

This point is important. Light cavalry, lightly equipped men on "uncovered" horses, are extremely rare in Edward I's reign and the first half of Edward II. As a fighting force they may be disregarded. Only on two occasions, mentioned above, did Edward I have as many as 400 light Irish hobelars, and then only for a few months. Thus when the chronicler of Falkirk, Walter of Hemingburgh, gives us 3000 heavy and 4000 light cavalry for that campaign, we can reject the figures. Much more readily can be rejected Barbour's 3000 heavy and 37,000 light for Bannockburn.

A systematic levy of hobelars began after Bannockburn, and of this we have documentary evidence. Cumberland and Westmoreland, raided by Bruce year by year after Bannockburn, raised light horse in self-defence to match the Scots who rode light on fell ponies. They were called "hobelars" because they had "hobby" horses, and there can be little doubt that their equipment, and it may be also their name, was in imitation of the Irish.

We are now in a position to consider the figures for Bannockburn. We must begin by stating that Andrew Lang was quite wrong when he said that both countries had had a year to prepare for the campaign. Documentary evidence is not lacking on this point, and Edward II had a bare two or three months in which to get ready. There was no regular feudal levy by consent of Parliament; the king simply called upon his barons to produce their contingents, and though the Earls of Lancaster and Warwick refused to serve in person because the war had not been sanctioned, they sent their men to represent them. It is thus assumed that a full feudal muster was made, and several writers have dwelt upon the fact to show that Edward had after all a large force of cavalry.

But luckily we have the Marshal's Register for 1310, when also a feudal muster was summoned, and the recalcitrant earls sent the barest minimum of men after the strictest interpretation of feudal custom. In 1310 Lancaster sent four knights and four *servientes*, Warwick one knight and 13 *servientes*, Oxford one knight and three *servientes*; Surrey and Arundel sent none in 1310, and if they sent a bare minimum in 1314 they would have been represented by about 15 and 10 horsemen respectively. Of the great barons only Lord Mortimer was conspicuously absent in 1314, and he sent one knight and four servientes in 1310. Therefore the numerical strength of these retinues would come to about 60 horsemen. We have no clue at all as to how many churchmen sent their feudal retinues in 1314; 27 bishops and abbots sent, between them, two knights and 152 *servientes* in 1310.

Turning from those who may have unwillingly contributed a few soldiers to those who served loyally and willingly, we have a little direct evidence. The "protections" as given in the Scottish Roll of the year show us 830 horse of all ranks, and this of course is a minimum figure. The Earl of Gloucester had protections for 131 followers; Aymer de Valence for 86, of whom at least six were bannerets and 20 knights; the two Despensers for 62; the Earl of Hereford for 45; Richard de Grey for 26; John Mowbray for 24; Henry Beaumont for 29; and Robert Clifford for 12, of which number, however, at least eight were knights. It is quite possible that the 830 represent a full total of 2000 or 2500. Now an absolutely contemporary English chronicler puts the total at 2000, of which 500 were raised by the Earl of Gloucester alone.

A contemporary Scottish rhymer. Abbot Bernard of Arbroath, is quoted by a much later chronicler as putting the English total at *millia ter quoque centum*, and this has been interpreted by different writers to mean 300,000 or 3100. If he really meant 3100 he was making a pretty good guess for a chronicler of the period. The Irish and foreigners in the campaign may be neglected. It is very easy to exaggerate the numbers of the Gascons who helped to garrison Edward's castles in Scotland, and such phrases as "the dead bodies of Gascons covered the plains" must be used with caution.

Certainly some Irish were summoned and shipping was provided for them, but there is no evidence that they were up at Bannockburn. Correct figures of the numbers of Gascons and Irish who are proved by documents to have been in Edward I's pay have been given above.

C. Infantry.

Horsemen could be raised in any part of England, where the baron or the professional captain of paid troops might choose. But foot were raised by Edwards I and II by counties;—except, indeed, the cross-bowmen, who were very few in numbers, never more than 350 and rarely more than 100 in any army, and who were chiefly in garrison in the castles. In the war of 1277 in Wales Edward I massed together 15,000 foot, but of these 9000 were South Welsh serving as his allies under their marcher lords against Llewelyn's North Welsh, and only 6000 were English.

Firstly it must be noted that this is the largest force of infantry that he ever collected together at one time and in one body in Wales. He soon broke the army up into smaller corps, and rarely had more than 5000 under his personal command, while detached bodies were serving in other directions. Secondly, the men were partly archers, partly foot spearmen; but choice bodies of a few hundreds were purely archers and were brigaded with the crossbowmen. Thirdly, they served for short spells, and relays came to relieve those in the field with startling rapidity.

The custom was for the king to summon foot only from the counties nearest to and most interested in the war, namely Lancashire, Cheshire, Shropshire and Staffordshire which had a sheriff in common, Herefordshire, and Gloucestershire. Only once did Lincolnshire send foot to Wales, and once Westmoreland. But Nottinghamshire and Derbyshire, also counties under one sheriff, steadily sent infantry to every war in Wales and almost every campaign in Scotland; these were not border counties, yet we expect to find keen fighters coming from Sherwood forest and the neighbourhood, whether pardoned outlaws or countrymen who had learnt archery from them, and though the real Robin Hood has never yet been discovered it is interesting to see that his county supplied good infantry. In a campaign in 1287 against the rebel Rhys ap Meredith an army of 10,600 foot was quickly raised, of whom 7000 were Welsh and the rest came from Cheshire, Shropshire, Herefordshire, and Nottinghamshire and Derbyshire.

When the war against Balliol began, Edward I according to the custom summoned foot from North England. But obviously they were not good soldiers, and he had to alter the custom. In the winter of 1297-8 a great force of 21,000 foot was collected from the North and from Wales; it seems to have been a rabble and was soon dismissed; 750 horse and 250 crossbows were also then serving. In 1298 the king summoned against Wallace 10,000 Welsh and 2000 men of Cheshire and Lancashire, evidently preferring his old allies and old enemies of Wales and his trusty men of the border of Wales to the inexperienced levies of Northumberland or Yorkshire; the archers of this levy won the Battle of Falkirk.

In succeeding years he had great difficulties in raising both horse, as we saw in the last section, and foot. In 1300 he summoned 16,000 from the North counties of England; 4000 appeared early in July, 9000 were present for a fortnight, and in August the number dropped to 5000; the men had deserted. There is no doubt of the fact. Edward issued proclamations against the deserters. In Wales he had never once had to do this.

In fact, the men of the counties bordering Wales and of Nottinghamshire and Derbyshire excepted, Englishmen then were not warlike. Just as in the eighteenth and nineteenth centuries we raised large numbers of German mercenaries to fight the French, and conquered India mostly by means of *sepoys* in our own service, so in Edward I's time most of the foot in an English Army were Welshmen. It was from Wales that the use of the bow was learnt, for in the first chapter we saw how Strongbow invaded Ireland with Norman horse and South Welsh bowmen. The border counties of Wales may have had in them men of partly Welsh blood, and probably owing to many border wars of which history has taken no account had naturally taken to fighting. Southerners never and midlanders rarely served, and the five northern counties had no stomach for war, did not like service, turned up in insufficient numbers, and constantly deserted.

It is extremely difficult to think of a Northumbrian or a Yorkshireman as a coward or a deserter, but the fact remains, and it may be said that the defeat of Bannockburn and the subsequent raids made by Bruce over the border year after year, when he levied blackmail upon clerics and laymen alike and spread a reign of terror down as far as York, forced the Englishman of these counties to be warlike, one might almost say, against his will. All this seems to be characteristic of the Anglo-Saxon race: it is slow to begin, it makes use of allies and foreigners when and where it can, needs a salutary lesson, in fact has to be forced to defend itself, back to the wall, and then at last becomes pugnacious.

And so it came to pass that after much slackness and refusal to fight in the days of Edward I and Edward II, after having suffered woe at the hands of Bruce's raiders, the men of the North Country at last warmed in self-defence; and, whereas they were abjectly cowed from 1314 down to 1327, they were able to defend themselves with considerable effect in 1346 when they alone won the Battle of Neville's Cross, whilst their king with the main army of the rest of England lay before Calais.

In this evolution of a good fighting infantry everything seems to depend upon the use of the efficient weapon. No army of Edward I or Edward II was entirely armed with bows, but obviously the proportion of bowmen to other foot was growing during these reigns, until all the English infantry at Crécy was bow-armed; and whereas the use of the bow was learnt from Wales and slowly caught on as an English weapon, in the days of Crécy it had become the English weapon par excellence, and it was the non-archer knife-armed Welshman who was looked down upon and paid the lower rate of twopence per day when the English archer drew threepence.

The reign of Edward II is the bad period in this history of the evolution of the English archer. Apparently Edward II himself did not believe in archers. In 1311 he sent writs to the sheriffs of all the counties of England to array and send to rendezvous at Roxburgh one man from each village. These are writs addressed to all the sheriffs of all the counties, and there is nothing said about the men being archers. Judging by a later year of his reign, 1322, one would suppose that he meant it to be a levy of foot spearmen. These writs indeed were cancelled, and therefore the year 1311 cannot be quoted as the first occasion when all the counties of the whole of England were summoned to Scotland, but the fact that the king issued these writs at all is of considerable importance.

In 1314 he first summoned foot on March 9th: 2000 archers from Yorkshire, 1000 from Nottinghamshire and Derbyshire, 1000 from Northumberland, and 500 from Lincolnshire, with bows and arrows and other competent arms; these writs were cancelled and, being cancelled, have not been printed in the official copy of the Scottish Rolls. On March 24th he summoned 21,540 foot, but we cannot possibly tell what proportion were expected to be bowmen. The levies evidently were being raised too slowly to suit him. His third writs of summons are dated May 27th. He says:

> We had ordered the men to be ready by a date already past. The enemy is striving to assemble great numbers of foot in strong and marshy places which it is very difficult for the cavalry to

reach. Therefore you are to exasperate and hurry up and compel the men to come.

The following is the list:

Yorkshire	4000	Glamorgan	500
Notts, and Derby	2000	Brecknock	200
Northumberland	2500	Abergavenny	200
Salop and Staffordshire	2000	The Mortimer Marches	300
Warwickshire and			
Leicestershire	500	Powys	500
Lancashire	500	Hope	40
Lincolnshire	3000	James de Pirar	200
The Bishop of Durham	1500	The Forest of Dean	100
North Wales	2000	Cheshire	500
South Wales	1000		

But of course we have no knowledge that, after the delays and with less than a month between these writs and the Battle of Bannockburn, the full number of 21,540 foot turned up. We can only say finally that the heavy cavalry of the campaign *may* have been 2500 strong, and the foot were *probably* about 15,000 if a proportion of those summoned appeared. It is not so much a bad guess as a gross blunder if it is considered that, because this number was summoned from certain counties of England and from Wales, therefore the total number from all the counties of England would have been about 40,000, for the other counties had never previously been called upon for a Scottish war unless we consider the cancelled writs of the year 1311.

Note. The references to the pay-rolls and horse-lists, which are among the Exchequer Accounts in the Public Record Office, may be found in my *Welsh Wars of Edward I.* The writs of summons are printed in the *Rotuli Scotiae* and *Parliamentary Writs* (Records Commission), and may be found under the dates given.

CHAPTER 3

Tactics Before Bannockburn

In medieval warfare, almost more strikingly than in other periods, success depended on combination. Horse unsupported by missile-armed foot could not break a steady stand of pikes. Unsupported pikemen were powerless against archers. And in their turn archers, surprised and taken in flank or rear, were powerless against horse. This is all so clear, and the experience of both Strongbow in Ireland and Richard in Palestine showed so strongly the need of combination, that it is almost amazing to find how the barons despised and neglected infantry. At Lewes and Evesham, though infantry were present, all the fighting fell on the horsemen. Moreover the mailed and mounted men were terribly awkward. It took a long time to dress them in line, and at Lewes Earl Simon alone was able to do this elementary work. They charged clumsily straight ahead, and one doubts if they could wheel at a trot. Certainly Edward I did his best in Wales and Scotland to introduce anew the much needed combination. Yet by no means all of his foot were archers. Curiously enough at both of the battles in Wales where combination triumphed Edward was not present in person.

In 1282 on the banks of the Yrfon, a tributary of the Wye near Builth, Roger l'Estrange in command of the men of Herefordshire and Shropshire came upon the army of Llewelyn. The English could not at first cross the river in face of resistance, but later got over unseen by a ford higher up and coming along the bank attacked the Welsh up hill. Llewelyn had been absent and was hurrying to the sound of battle, when a certain Stephen Frankton ran him through the body with his lance, not knowing who he was. The Welsh were leaderless:

But they stood in their troops on the brow of the hill awaiting their lord and prince, but in vain. As our men mounted the hill, the Welsh shot their arrows and darts upon them. But through our archers, who were fighting by concert in between our cavalry, many of them fell, all the more so because they stood up boldly expecting Llewelyn. Finally our cavalry gained the top of the hill, and cut them down or put them to flight. (Walter of Hemingburgh.)

Early in 1295 during Madoc's rising Edward I was being besieged in Conway Castle, and the Earl of Warwick was hastening to his relief. At Maes Madoc, about 18 miles south of Conway:

Warwick, hearing that the Welsh had assembled in great strength in a plain between two forests, with a picked force of cavalry with crossbowmen and archers pushed on by night and surrounded them on all sides. They rested the butts of their spears on the ground, and presenting the points when the English horse charged held them off. But the earl posted a crossbowman between each pair of horsemen, (or an archer, for the number of crossbows was very small,) and when many of the spearmen had been brought down by the bolts, the horse charged again and defeated them with greater slaughter than, it is thought, had ever been suffered by them in past times. (Nicholas Trivet.)

A comparison of these two battles shows that the English tactics were the same at each. At Builth some at least of the Welsh were archers of the South, but at Maes Madoc they were all spearmen of the North. This was a characteristic difference between North and South Welshmen, and is mentioned by Gerald who chronicled Strongbow's wars.

In the Scottish war of 1298, before the Battle of Falkirk, two things have to be noticed. Firstly, Edward I's army was much straitened for want of victuals, which he had hoped to receive by sea, and he was on the point of retreat towards Edinburgh when he was told that Wallace was preparing to attack him; the difficulty of feeding an army in Scotland appears in every war. Secondly, the Welsh levies, who formed the bulk of Edward's foot, in a drunken brawl killed some English, and several of them were killed in revenge. Edward, warned that they would desert to the Scots, replied, "Let them go; they are both our enemies, and we will be revenged on them together." So says the chronicler. But a large proportion of his Welsh foot were from the marches which had always been loyal to him. In the battle:

The Scots formed all their people in four bodies in rings, on hard ground on one side (of a morass) near Fawkirk; their spearmen had their spears sloping upwards, and they stood shoulder to shoulder with their faces outwards. Between the rings were spaces where stood their archers, and in the rear were their cavalry. . . The earls who commanded the first English brigade, Norfolk the Earl Marshal, Hereford (the Constable), and Lincoln, advanced in a straight line not knowing that there was a lake between; so they had to draw off to the westwards and were somewhat delayed. The Bishop of Durham (Antony Bek), with the second brigade of 36 banners, was aware of the lake and turned to the east to pass round it. As the men were *pushing on too fast so as to have the honour of attacking first*, the bishop bade them wait for the king and the third brigade, but Ralph Basset of Drayton cried out, 'Mind your own business and say mass; we soldiers will do our proper work.'

So they hastened and charged the nearest ring of the Scots, and the three earls with the first brigade charged on the other side. Soon the Scots horse fled without striking a blow, except a few who were officers of the rings of infantry called schiltrons. . . . And the Scots archers of Selkirk Forest, tall and handsome men, being killed with their commander, our men concentrated their attack on the spearmen in their rings who were like a thick wood, and *could not force their way in because of the number of spears*, though they struck and stabbed some on the outside. But *our foot shot at them with arrows*, and some with stones which lay there in plenty. So many were slain and the front ranks pushed back on the rear ranks in confusion, and then our horse broke in and routed them. (Hemingburgh, vol. II.)

The narrative speaks for itself. The English lords rode jealous and without discipline. The schiltrons of Scots, just like the Welsh at Maes Madoc, were quite able to beat horse alone, but not to stand up to archers, whom they could not attack in turn without losing their formation. The English and Welsh foot were obviously in the rear at first, and did not come up till the first charges of horse had been repulsed. The brigades (*acies*, or *battles*) were of horse alone, and the foot were massed separately. The handful of Scots horse were powerless, and there is no need to call them traitors. The Scots archers were never numerous. Each of these points requires consideration, because

Bruce evidently took the lesson to heart; at Bannockburn he drew up his more scientifically, kept his small force of cavalry in reserve out of sight so as to launch it suddenly on the English archers, and had a certain number of archers in his own ranks who were far from useless.

Ralph Basset, the boaster, does not seem to have done much in the battle after all. He is registered in a horse-list as serving in the paid cavalry with two knights and nine *servientes*, but not one of their horses was damaged. Of other leaders of paid cavalry, Thomas of Lancaster, Edward I's nephew and Edward II's bitter enemy, lost 11 horses in a squadron of 45, Aymer de Valence lost 5 out of 50, Hugh Despenser 8 out of 50, Robert Clifford 10 out of 35, and Henry Beaumont 4 out of 10. All these, except Lancaster, were present at Bannockburn. Yet not one of them took to heart the lesson of Falkirk, and Clifford and Beaumont were most conspicuous at Bannockburn by their headlong charge of horse unsupported by archers against Moray's ring of pikes. Also at Falkirk in the retinue of despenser rode a squire named Giles of Argentine; we shall find him at Bannockburn, and in the interval he won a reputation as a crusader and the third most famous knight in Christendom.

In 1302 the French fought the Flemings at Courtrai, mailed cavalry against foot pikemen, and to the surprise of Europe they were beaten. Here were the knights and heroes of chivalry humbled by plebeian townsmen. Yet the English lords still refused to learn the lesson. On the contrary one of our best chroniclers, Gray of Heton, tells us that Bruce did learn, and that he formed up his schiltrons at Bannockburn in imitation of the Flemings. Gray is really wrong. Doubtless Bruce knew about Courtrai, but Falkirk was fought four years before that, and if he imitated any one he imitated Wallace. In truth he had no need to learn even from Wallace, or Wallace from the spearmen of North Wales, or the Flemings or Swiss from the Scots. A long shaft of wood with an iron head has been used by foot in all ages. It is nature's weapon for poor or untrained men against professional mounted men. Welsh, Scots, Flemings, Swiss, all these could make an impenetrable hedge.

But a stand of pikes cannot easily manoeuvre; men must be drilled to advance, or to form up rapidly in face of a surprise attack, when they are carrying long and heavy poles. The merit of Bruce is that he did train his Scots to advance and not only to meet standing a charge of horse; so did Philip and Alexander of Macedon of old, and the Swiss leaders at Morgarten and Morat; so too did Cromwell in an age when half the foot were still pikemen, though the other half had muskets. Wallace's schiltrons were rings of men unable to counter-charge; Bruce's schiltrons in the main Battle of Bannockburn were lines which charged, slowly it may be, but effectively and steadily, though in the fight overnight Moray formed a ring to resist Clifford and Beaumont.

The word, variously written as schiltron, schiltrome, schiltrum, meaning shield-wall, is found in the English chroniclers Hemingburgh and Gray. Barbour does not use it of the Scots themselves, but only of the nine brigades of English horse who were crowded together so that they were unmanageable; "bot in a schiltrum it semyt thai war all and some."

We may take it then that the secret of Bruce's tactics was his train-ing of his schiltrons to advance in an orderly formation en echelon, while he kept such of his light cavalry as he needed where they would not be out-numbered and useless. He established a tradition that Scots should take the offensive, and they did so at Dupplin Moor and Halidon Hill and Neville's Cross with disastrous results, for the new English formation of archers and dismounted knights was much too powerful for them after Bruce's death. But without anticipating the English reform which avenged Bannockburn, let us by way of contrast turn again to the medieval baron. Whether English or French, he was greedy of fighting but ambitious to be himself alone in action; he was practically untrained and unable to manoeuvre; he found his enemy and rode at him without any science.

He wanted to be ahead, not only of the mass of English or Welsh foot whom he despised, but also of his own comrades-in-arms. He nearly spoilt Edward I's chances at Falkirk, and quite ruined Edward II at Bannockburn. He needed the lesson of defeat. The second Edward was no coward, but he was no general, and the English went into battle unprepared and untrained, as if a science of tactics were unnecessary. He was the only possible commander-in-chief, yet had no influence over Gloucester or Hereford. He simply led his army into a trap where a river was at his back, where he had no room to handle his superior forces, even if he had the ability and they the training, where the foot were mostly out of action and the horsemen got jammed into a mob before the pikes of Bruce's steady Scots.

Note. The chronicles of Hemingburgh and Trivet are in the English Historical Society's publications.

CHAPTER 4

The Historians of Bannockburn

The most celebrated and most often quoted historian of Bannockburn is John Barbour of Aberdeen, but he wrote at the end of the 14th century about sixty years after the war. It is quite notorious how people who draw upon their memory only make mistakes, not only because it is difficult to remember, but because the facts are already lost in the mists of antiquity, or at least appear out of proportion at the time when the historian records what he thinks that they were. We can only criticise such a man as Barbour in two ways. Did he use contemporary authorities and understand them when he used them? and is his work, as judged by internal evidence, consistent with itself and with the accounts of other historians? Now we know that there were contemporary rhymers at work on Bannockburn. We have already quoted Abbot Bernard, but from the lines attributed to him we cannot say that he is responsible for any valuable information.

There was also a certain poor Carmelite Friar, by name Robert Baston, who was celebrated as the chief English rhymer of the day, and was taken to Scotland by Edward II to write a poem in honour of the coming victory; being made prisoner by Bruce he was compelled to write a poem on the defeat. The lines given to us as Baston's in another later Scottish chronicle, called the *Scotichronicon*, begun by Fordun and continued by Bower about a century after the battle, give us nothing definite but one fact, *viz.* that Bruce really did dig little pits or pots in front of his army.

Barbour is the chief authority for the existence of the pits, and two Englishmen, Geoffrey Baker of Swinbroke, and Abbot Burton of Meaux, repeat the story, both of them obviously from Baston. Also one line of Baston reads: *Anglicolae quasi Coelicolae splendore nitescunt,* and Barbour says how the English army shone like angels, and Baker, remembering the old jest, speaks of his fellow countrymen as Angles and not Angels. Baston is the only first-hand authority that we know to have been used by Barbour, and what Barbour obtained from him amounts to very little.

But when we apply the second criticism to Barbour we are bound to state that, although we are strongly prejudiced against a man who wrote 60 years after the event, his account is entirely consistent with itself. He never contradicts himself; many of his statements are completely borne out by the English contemporary authorities, and a literal interpretation of Barbour enables us to understand the general plan of the campaign. A historian, wishing to get at the truth, is amply justified in taking Barbour's account and testing it step by step against the shorter English accounts, and it will then be seen not only that we have an intelligible story, but also that the various English statements fall into place like bits of a puzzle when once the key is found. Of course there is another reason for prejudice; Barbour is one of the worst statisticians and is chiefly responsible for the myth of an army of 100,000.

But he himself supplies the antidote; he gives 40,000 as the figure of all the English cavalry, but 3000 as the number of the "covered" horse; only the 3000 need be counted, and the exaggeration is not very bad, while the 37,000 may be rejected altogether. The main point is this; if we get from him an intelligent account which satisfies military critics, it is probably a true account; if he was inventing, he would be sure to make mistakes. But his account is intelligent, and we can easily put away our prejudice against him on the score of his absurd figures.

Of the English writers by far the most important is Sir Thomas Gray of Heton, son of another Sir Thomas Gray who fought at Bannockburn and was taken prisoner, but was afterwards ransomed and defended Norham Castle against Bruce. The writer was also Governor of Norham in later days and was also taken prisoner by the Scots, and when in prison in Edinburgh he tells us that he read several chronicles in French and in English, in prose and in verse, which encouraged him to write his own history. He calls this the *Scalacronica*, because he dreamt that he ascended a ladder to the top of a high wall, beyond which he saw various things going on. It is the work therefore of a soldier and the son of a soldier who had actually been in the battle. It has been edited by the Maitland Club, but is unluckily out of print. Sir Herbert Maxwell (Maclehose, Glasgow) has issued an English translation.

The so-called *Chronicle of Lanercost* was written by a succession of Franciscans of Carlisle, and the particular section which deals with Bannockburn was written by a contemporary who quotes his authority:

> This I was told by somebody worthy to be believed, who was present there himself and saw it.

It has also been edited for the Maitland Club, and translated by Sir Herbert.

The *Vita Edwardi Secundi*, edited by Bishop Stubbs (Rolls Series), is almost contemporary, and seems to be the work of a monk of Malmesbury Abbey, who was writing up to 1325. It is a fairly long piece of work and gives us many important facts. For instance it is here that we have the definite statement that the English cavalry were 2000 strong of which the Earl of Gloucester led at his own cost 500. There is a short reference to Bannockburn in a good contemporary chronicle which comes from Bridlington Priory in Yorkshire, and a slightly longer account comes from John of Trokelowe, one of the many chronicler monks of St Albans. Towards the end of the century Abbot Burton of Meaux wrote a history, mostly of his own Abbey, but also of general matters of interest; he was clearly using some older material, and if we cannot consider him as contemporary, at least he represents the English point of view which had become traditional. All these are to be found in the Rolls Series.

Lastly, we have to consider Geoffrey Baker of Swinbroke. He is our chief authority on military matters in the Hundred Years' War. It is not only that he has written on Crécy and Poitiers much more intelligently than Froissart; he also understood, or was coached by somebody who understood, the evolution of the Edwardian tactics of combining foot and horse. Baker deliberately tells us that at Crécy the archers were posted on the wings where they poured their arrows like lightning into the flanks of the attacking French cavalry, whereas at Bannockburn the bulk of the archers were useless in rear of their own cavalry.

Now some of Baker's statements about Bannockburn are obviously wrong, probably because he took the facts literally from Friar Baston, and embroidered or wrote them out without a critical examination. For instance he talks about the English Army glittering, as Baston tells us, and then adds wrongly on his own authority that the English had the sun in their eyes. He has entirely neglected the preliminary fighting on the first day of the battle. But it is impossible to pass over him as a chief authority, for it is absurd to consider him as the best writer to follow for Crécy and reject him for Bannockburn. His chronicle has been edited by Sir E. M. Thompson (Clarendon Press).

Modern historians, one feels as one reads them, have had some trouble to explain Bannockburn. Each one chooses an authority, it may be Gray or Baker or the Lanercost chronicler, and seems to despair of fitting in the details given by others. The main fact is plain enough, the rout of horse by foot, and that alone seems to be essential. Yet we want to understand more, and in particular from the English side we want to see how the nation was so badly humbled in 1314 which was so brilliantly successful on another scene in 1346. The typical description of Bannockburn is not convincing, and one has felt in trying to describe it oneself that one has not been convincing. The best account has been that of Sir Evelyn Wood, who was years ago an officer in garrison at Stirling, frequently visited the reputed field of battle, and left some notes which ultimately came into the hands of Sir Herbert Maxwell. His is a soldier's description of the battle. He asked himself where Moray must have been posted before he fought Clifford, where and how the main force of English cavalry crossed the burn, where the archers came into action.

But there is this flaw. Sir Evelyn only knew of the reputed site, and every other historian has taken this as the only possible site, even Andrew Lang whose flair is so well known. Much of the chronicled evidence will not fit into any account of the battle fought on this site. It has only been the "traditional" site since Nimmo wrote his *History of Stirlingshire* in the late 18th century. We all know that "I learnt it at school and therefore it is true," or "the guide-book says so," is no argument. This is the same argument as that which still binds some people to the 100,000. Yet we have been slaves, and tried to make the evidence fit the site, and not the site the evidence. Suddenly Mr W. M. Mackenzie chooses a different site and all is plain. And how does he break the spell? He simply takes Barbour and Gray, the only two authorities who do precisely give any statement at all, follows them literally, locates the battle on the Carse, and at once all is plain.

Mr Round in an article in his *Commune of London* has blamed Professor Oman's account, or rather his various accounts in different books. Certainly it is difficult to follow an historian who in one version puts the archers in the front, and in another in the rear, in the one case following the Lanercost chronicle and in the other Baker. Yet this is but typical of many historians who have found the battle difficult to explain. But Professor Oman in his *Art of War in the Middle Ages* has made some serious mistakes besides those of inconsistency, and one must point them out, because others follow him and perpetuate the error. He puts the English army as 10,000 strong in horse and 40,000 in foot, and then assumes that 30,000 of these were incomparable archers. This he does by adding 7000 light horse to the 3000 "covered "horse mentioned by Barbour, and by arguing that if Edward summoned 21,540 foot from some counties a gross total of 40,000 came from all England.

Each fallacy has been exposed above. Worse still, he gives a plan of the battle in which horse and foot are brigaded together in each of the ten "battles" of which Barbour tells us. But Barbour clearly states that each of the ten were of horse alone, and the combination of archers with dismounted cavalrymen was the post-Bannockburn reform which made Crécy possible. Let us try to imagine the English going into action according to this plan; in first line three bodies of horse, and foot immediately behind them; in second line the same formation; in third line the same formation; the result would be confusion so hopeless and ludicrous that one can hardly believe even Edward II at Bannockburn to have been so crazy as to array his army in such a way. It is a minor detail that Barbour divides the ten into a van and nine behind on a side, and Professor Oman depicts nine in three lines in front and the tenth as a reserve. This plan has been copied into other histories as if it were perfect.

CHAPTER 5

Sunday, June 23rd, 1314

The *Chronicle of Lanercost* begins to describe the campaign in words imputing blame to the king who was so soon to be defeated.

He drew near to Scotland with a very fine and large army. But the Earl of Lancaster, and other earls who were of his party—except the strict service which they owed to the king in war—remained at home, because the king had refused to come to terms with them and to carry out what he had promised. And whereas his noble father Edward I on his way to war had been wont to visit the saints of England, to make them rich offerings, and to commend himself to their prayers, giving bountiful alms also to monasteries and to the poor, he did nothing of the sort, *but coming with great pomp and curious retinue he seized upon the goods of the monasteries en route*, and by word and deed acted to the prejudice and injury of the saints. Therefore it is not surprising that *defeat and everlasting shame came upon him and his army, as indeed was prophesied at the time.*

In the same way Robert of Reading, a monk of Westminster, writes in *Flores Historiarum*:

Edward allowed his army on its march through the lands of the religious and other churchmen to carry off like robbers sheep and cattle and horses and whatever they fancied.

This, of course, is with a purpose. A tale of defeat has as its prelude an accusation of wrong done to the Church. Yet any soldier of the period would have agreed that the king had the right to requisition supplies and transport from those who could not fight; friar and monk had no right to the king's protection if they grudged payment for it.

We continue from the *Vita Edwardi Secundi*. After emphasising that the war was without consent of Parliament, Edward merely relying on the voluntary services of Gloucester and Hereford and Pembroke and many barons who had turned to loyalty in disgust at Gaveston's murder, though five earls sent their strict quotas only, the author continues:

"Six or seven days before the feast of St John he left Berwick with *more than 2000 armed horse and a very numerous infantry*. There were enough men there to march through the whole of Scotland, and some thought that if all Scotland were collected together it could not resist the king's army. *Never in our time did such an army quit England*. The multitude of carts stretched out in a line would have taken up twenty leagues. The king, in his confidence, hastened day by day towards his goal. Short time was allowed for sleep, shorter for meals. Horses, horsemen, and infantry, overcome by toil and want of food, are not to be blamed for their failure in battle."

To this we can add that the route taken was from the Tweed up Lauderdale and beneath Soutra Hill to Edinburgh, for on June 18 Edward addressed from "Soltre" a letter to the Archbishop of Canterbury. (Bain, vol. iii. No. 365.) Here, says Mr Mackenzie, stood a hospital for travellers since the 12th century; and a main modern road traverses Lauderdale between the Tweed and Edinburgh. Therefore we have proof that the army marched inland and not by the difficult coast from Berwick to Dunbar. This was an open and thinly populated moorland, and often enough on other occasions the Scots had no need to fight, but let their foes wear themselves out and starve. But now the long line of carts at least bore victuals enough for the first few weeks of the campaign. There was a definite objective, Stirling. Bruce preferred to make his stand in the woods through which ran the road to Stirling, and made no attempt to harass the army struggling in such hot haste up Lauderdale. When Edinburgh was reached we may suppose that a halt was made to allow the rear and the baggage train to close up, for that such an army straggled is self-evident. Barbour tells us that on Saturday June 22 it marched the whole distance from Edinburgh to Falkirk, twenty miles and a bit more, a somewhat difficult feat for even much better disciplined troops.

But there is no reason to doubt what Barbour says about Bruce's plans, and we can continue with him for our guide. The rendezvous for the Scots was the Torwood, the forest north of Falkirk, through which the English would have to pass by the medieval road; it is quite possible that a Roman road once ran from Antonine's wall to cross the Forth at Stirling, thence on to Ardoch camp, but skilled authorities profess they are unable to trace it now. There then Bruce arrayed his army; he himself took the rear; the van he gave to Thomas son of Randolph, Earl of Moray, his nephew; two other brigades, or "battles" in medieval language, he assigned respectively to his brother Edward Bruce, and to young Walter Stewart, who was directed by James Douglas. This order is of some importance, and it was the order for retreat and not for battle. Moray was leading the retreat, and Bruce was covering the army by his rear-guard against the English advance, while Edward Bruce and Douglas were behind and to the side of the van. It was a sort of diamond formation:

```
         Moray
Douglas          Edward
         Bruce
```

Such was the array at least on the Friday, and on Saturday, as word came of the English march from Edinburgh, they all fell back to the next forest, the New Park, which covered Stirling to the south.

The great rock of Stirling, like a wedge lying on its side, overhangs the Forth a few miles below the tidal limit. The town and castle guard the bridge, the first bridge over the river as one goes up, at a point very far inland. To this fact the place owes its fame. It commands a wide view to east and west, eastwards over the loops of the Forth as it twists and twines, westwards up the fertile valley which lies between the Campsie Fells and the Ochils. The Highlands shut in the view, and on most days Ben Ledi and Ben Lomond can be seen. Such a fortress in the waist of Scotland, so far inland, and a bridge-place, has ever been of great military importance.

Bruce, we are told by Barbour, deliberately chose the New Park for his stand. An upland rises from the north bank of the Bannock and the road to Stirling climbs up to strike through the Park. From the front of the position the approach of the English could be clearly seen; a frontal attack could be prepared against; a flanking movement to reach Stirling by the flat ground of the Carse to the east could be also foreseen. So Bruce himself was ready to protect the "entry" of the road into the wood, with his brother Edward near him; Moray was posted further back near the Kirk of St Ninian, with Douglas in support, and the kirk stands near the sharp edge of the high ground beneath which is the Carse, stretching to the Forth. From all the de-

FROM STIRLING CHURCH TOWER LOOKING EASTWARDS DOWN THE FORTH, AND SHOWING THE WINDINGS OF THE RIVER.

From Stirling Church Tower looking north-westwards, and showing the Highlands beyond the Castle.

tailed accounts, Barbour's, Gray's, the *Lanercost Chronicle* and the *Vita*, we find such frequent references to the wood that it is certain that the New Park covered most of the upland. The Scottish Army was hidden, ready to move out to meet the English, whether the advance came from the front or by the flank.

Posted here Bruce, on the Saturday, ordered to be dug the famous pits or "pottis." Where were they and what part did they play in the battle? The prime authority is the friar and rhymer, Robert Baston. The words are:

> A device full of woe is formed for the horses' feet, hollow, with spikes, that they may not pass without fall. The commons dig ditches that on them the cavalry may trip.

That is all. The English chronicler. Baker of Swinbroke, takes Baston's fact and builds up a story of a long ditch or ditches, singular or plural in different parts of his narrative, three feet wide and three deep, covered with hurdles and screened with grass, "constructed I will not say deceitfully but cannily." He takes another fact, the tripping of the English cavalry in the bed of the burn when they broke and fled after Monday's main battle. He puts the two facts together and tells us that on Monday's charge they tripped in the ditches. Abbot Burton of Meaux quotes straight from Baston:

> Iron spikes had been placed in hollows under the ground so that both horse and foot might trip." One can say from Baker and Burton that tradition in England, in the generations after Bannockburn, considered the pits an essential feature of the battle. In Tytler's *History of Scotland* (3rd edition 1845, vol. i), is given the evidence of a certain Lieutenant Campbell, who visited the accepted site of the battle at a time when the marshes bordering the Bannock were being drained. He saw a number of circular holes about 18 inches deep, very close to one another, with a sharp pointed stake in the centre of each. The stakes were in a state of decomposition. . . There were some swords, spear-heads, horse-shoes, horse-hair (the latter generally mixed with a whitish animal matter resembling tallow) found in them.

The statement is precise, but is not corroborated by anybody. Were no Scots a century ago keen enough to follow up the question and see if Campbell was right? His evidence is mentioned in the first edition of Tytler in 1828, disappears from the second, is given at length in his own words in the third, and again disappears from later editions. The pits, he says, were at the western end of Halbert Marsh, near the Bannock, and it seems—for Campbell does not write clearly—that they swept round from the marsh along the *western* foot of Coxet Hill; *i.e.* just where Bruce did *not* kill Bohun, and where the evidence is very clear that there was no fighting on Sunday. It remains that Bruce *may* have dug holes anticipating an attack in this direction. But the account is suspicious, for we know nothing of Campbell, and, though he may have honestly believed that he had found the pots, he has no warrant. So let us go back to Barbour. We have a more precise statement from him than from Baston.

The pots were "in a playne feld by the way. . .; on ather syde the way weill braid it was pottit." The holes were thick together like a wax-comb. Evidently the place indicated was the ground on either side of the road, where the frontal attack might be expected, and where indeed Bohun did attack on the Sunday. Nothing could be clearer. But the curious thing is that Barbour makes no mention of any harm done by the pots on either the Sunday or the Monday. They were dug, and being dug had nothing to do with subsequent fighting. Baker alone speaks of the cavalry tripping on the Monday, the others only of a trap laid but not operative.

Another Bannockburn incident is almost certainly a myth. Barbour says that, when he took up his position, Bruce sent the camp-followers, not to Gillies' Hill, nor to any hill at all, but "to ane vale," *i.e.* one of the hollows below Coxet Hill. Mr Mackenzie suggests that the famous lull may take its name from some family of the common name of Gillies, whereas the Celtic word "gillies" is not to be expected in this part of Scotland and is not in the language spoken by either Bruce or Barbour. It was easy in later days to invent a location for the camp-followers on a hill so conveniently named, and so the myth was begun and has been adopted by everybody since.

Let us stand today on the high ground above the farm called "Foot o' Green." We are on the English side of the valley, our faces to the north. The Bannock runs below from west to east; its banks are in places low, but beyond rises the upland before mentioned which is about the 180 foot contour; to west and east the northern bank rises steep, and would be quite impossible for heavy cavalry. Behind the upland to our left is the well-wooded Gillies' Hill, in the centre Coxet Hill with Stirling Castle showing above in middle distance, to our right the Carse and glimpses of the Forth. Against the sky are the

Ochils with Wallace's "Abbey Craig" as a sentinel in front, and away to the north-west the higher mountains. Ben Ledi peeps over the shoulder of Gillies' Hill. It is a fair view. But the old conditions were very different. The bed of the Bannock is now farmed to the edge, and a mill-stream runs off the main stream of the burn to meet it again lower down; the water is today controlled and kept in its place.

In old days there were swamps in places, Halbert Bog and Milton Bog, between the burn and the foot of the upland. Mr Mackenzie does not believe this. But we have the evidence of Lieut. Campbell that the land was being drained in the early 19th century; Professor Oman says he has seen 18th century maps showing the swamps; old citizens of Stirling have told the present writer that there used to be swamp and water where now is the bowling-green beneath Borestone Brae, and that they used to skate there. True, the battle was fought in midsummer, and the weather was hot, for Barbour says that the Scots sweated with their efforts. But if there were swamps down in the Carse, as Mr Mackenzie tells us, why not also near the Bannock? especially as Mr Mackenzie makes no allowance for the artificial millstream which now pens in the water. The point is of importance, for, if Monday's battle took place here, the English cavalry could only have crossed on a very narrow front in places between the swamps. He thinks that Monday's battle was not fought here, no more do I; but one reason to my mind for putting the battle elsewhere is the difficulty of a passage here by the cavalry, which is Sir Evelyn Wood's chief contribution to the elucidation of the battle.

Secondly, and far more important than the question of swamps, comes the fact that the upland, today, (as at first publication), open, in 1314 was wooded. That the New Park covered nearly all the ground where most writers have located the battle is clear. It was argued a few paragraphs back on Barbour's evidence that Bruce chose the position for the very reason that it was wooded, so that his army was hidden. The chroniclers are quite definite in their language. The Scots issued from the wood unexpectedly, both on Sunday and on Monday.

Three roads now cross the burn and climb the slope to meet near St Ninian's Kirk. Which of them, if any, marks the direction of the old road it would be hard to say, but the general line of straightness from Falkirk to Stirling seems to indicate the middle one of the three; it passes east of and below "Foot o' Green" farm, crosses both the burn itself and the mill-stream, and mounts to the east of the borestone. The oldest map that I have seen in the British Museum, though on a small scale, gives the general direction. Along it let us imagine that Edward's van advanced.

Let us go back to our chroniclers. Sir Thomas Gray wrote:

Sir Philip Mowbray—Governor of Stirling Castle—met the king three leagues from the castle on Sunday, the Eve of St John, and said that there was no reason why he should come any nearer to effect a rescue; *he also told him how the enemy had blocked all the narrow paths through the wood*. But the young soldiers did not halt, but pushed on. The van, led by Gloucester, entered on the road through the park, and were soon thrown back by the Scots who held the road, and Sir Peter Montfort was slain it is said by Bruce's own hand with an axe.

Every other writer gives this honour to Henry Bohun, but the mistake does not lessen our respect for Gray's narrative.

In the *Vita Edwardi Secundi* we read:

The Earls of Gloucester and Hereford led the van. On Sunday, the Eve of St John, having already passed through a forest— the Torwood—and drawing near to Stirling, *they saw some Scots scattered near a wood*—the New Park—and apparently in retreat. Henry Bohun with some Welsh troops pursued them to the entry of the wood, in hope to find Bruce there and kill or capture him. Suddenly *Bruce appeared out of the wood*, and Henry seeing the Scots in great numbers turned his horse. But Bruce broke his head open with an axe. Then there was a sharp fight, in which Gloucester was unhorsed, Clifford was forced to flee, and as our men pursued the Scots (*sic*) many fell on both sides.

Here too is an inaccuracy, for Clifford fled on another side of the field, but the narrative is not spoilt thereby. Henry Bohun was, of course, a kinsman of the Earl of Hereford, and his name occurs in the list of those who had "protections" in Hereford's retinue. Robert of Reading, in the *Flores Historiarum*, contributes an interesting sentence, though otherwise he says nothing about the battle:

A mad rivalry broke out between Gloucester and Hereford about the control of the army and the office of constable. The king, in contempt of Hereford, gave the office to Gloucester, though belonging by hereditary right to Hereford and his line.

Naturally enough Edward preferred Gloucester, because Hereford had been contumacious and refused to attend the feudal levy in 1310.

Naturally also Hereford resented it, and the impetuous attack now was caused by jealous riding. Their fathers had been rebellious against Edward I as well as personal rivals. But Gloucester had been brought over to Edward II's side and was made Constable. It was unpardonable folly for Edward II to let such rivals ride together in the van.

Barbour's details of Bohun's charge upon Bruce who was mounted on "ane gray palfray litill and joly," Bruce's dexterous swerve, the terrific blow which killed Bohun, and his moan over his "hand-ax-schaft" that he had broken, are familiar. It must be added that Barbour says the Scots then charged forward and overtook and slew a few English, but their horses' feet saved the rest of the van. Also Edward Bruce debouched in rear of Robert. It was in fact a serious action between the van of one army and the rear of the other, but the truth of this is lost by those who only look at the romantic side of the king's personal duel.

Meanwhile Clifford and Beaumont with a body of horse crossed the Bannock and skirted the Park to the east, or else they made a wide detour beyond the present little town of Bannockburn; at least they were out of sight of Moray and his men posted near St Ninian's Kirk. Bruce blamed Moray and told him "that ane rose of his chaplet was faldyn," and as he had chosen the New Park on purpose because he could see the English, whether they should make a frontal attack like Bohun, or should try to outflank like Clifford, very naturally his condemnation was strong. The Lanercost chronicler assumes that Moray deliberately allowed them to ride round him:

> . . . . .until Clifford was some distance away, and then he and his men showed themselves, and cutting them off from the centre charged upon them, killing some and routing the rest.

Of the place of fighting there can be no doubt at all. It was "neuth the kirk. . . to the playn feld." Clifford had indeed turned the Scots' position, and had a clear way before him to the castle. But when *Moray appeared from the wood* with 500 spearmen on foot, the English preferred to fight rather than effect a formal rescue of the castle. They formed up to charge, but first gave the Scots time to form their national ring, even as Wallace drew up his rings at Falkirk. The "hedge-hog" or "hyrcheoune" of pikes corresponded to the hollow square of muskets against cavalry. The English could not break in, they only impaled their horses on the pikes, they had no archers in attendance to shoot down the Scots, and vainly threw darts and knives, swords and maces, at their steady foes. Douglas, whose brigade supported Moray, begged leave of Bruce to move up. But already Moray was beginning to advance on the baffled horsemen, and the sight of Douglas only completed the rout. Yet Barbour says definitely that the fight lasted a long time, beginning before Bruce's affair with Bohun and ending after it, and that the Scots sweated much and were weary. Barbour gives 800 horse under three bannerets as the number of Clifford's command.

But we have a much more competent authority than Barbour, namely Sir Thomas Gray, whose father was in the charge and was dragged in on foot into the ring as a prisoner. He puts the number at 300 horsemen. He makes Beaumont responsible for giving Moray time to form up, not Clifford. He says nothing of Douglas moving up. But otherwise he shows how excellent was Barbour's information:

> Meanwhile Robert Lord Clifford and Henry Beaumont with 300' men-at-arms rode round the wood on the other side towards the castle, and *held the open fields*. Thomas Randolph, Earl of Moray and nephew of Bruce, who was in command of the Scots' van, had heard that his uncle had driven back the English on the other side, and thought that he would like to have his share of the fighting; *so he issued from the wood with his division*, and took up a position in the open towards the two English lords. 'Let us give ground a little,' said Beaumont; 'let them come on; give them space!'—In the usual quarrel of words, as in many medieval battles, Beaumont taunted Gray, the author's father, for cowardice. Then Gray spurred his horse, and Sir William Dayncourt did the same, and they charged right into the enemy; Dayncourt was killed, and Gray taken prisoner, his horse being speared and himself dragged in on foot by the Scots, who totally routed the two lords. *Some of the English fled to the castle*, and some to the king's main army, which had retired from the road through the wood.

Baker, we have seen, is silent on the Sunday's fighting. The *Vita Edwardi Secundi* only mentions Bohun's attack, and seems to imply that Clifford was routed on that side. John of Trokelowe says shortly that:

> . . . .when tents had been pitched, some of the English rode in among the wedges of the Scots and attacked them fiercely. But they resisting manfully killed many English nobles that day, and the English, bitter because of their repulse, vowed to be

revenged on the morrow or die.

Where did the English pass the night? Every modern writer has assumed that they encamped to the south of the Bannock. But Mr Mackenzie says that they encamped across the Bannock in the Carse, in the loop which that tributary makes with the Forth. And his evidence is simple, just the plain statements of Barbour and Gray. These are the only two authorities who tell us where the encampment was; they are our best authorities on the one or the other side. The inference is plain, and we have no right to doubt them. Yet we wonder that nobody before Mr Mackenzie has taken them at their word. Gray wrote:

> The main army had come to a plain towards the waters of Forth *beyond Bannockburn*, a bad and deep watery marsh. There the English encamped and passed the night.

Barbour is equally precise;

> They harboured them that night down *in the Carse* (Kers) . . . and, for in the Carse were pools, houses and thatch they broke and bore to make bridges where they might pass; and some say that the folk in the castle, when night fell, bore doors and windows with them, so that they had before day bridged the pools, so that they were passed over every one and had taken the hard field on horse.

Had Gray alone written *outre Bannockburn* might possibly be taken to mean, as Andrew Lang thought, "on the side opposite to the Scots," Gray's father being their prisoner. Corroborated by Barbour he must be supposed to indicate the side opposite to the English line of advance, which is the natural meaning of the passage. The pools, Mr Mackenzie reminds us, are where the English baggage was bogged and captured by Wallace after the Battle of Stirling Bridge.

Lastly, how did they pass the night? Without sleep, say most chroniclers. Barbour shows that he understood things much better than has usually been thought; from his words quoted above we see that he knew that an army of 15,000 or 18,000 men with a great baggage-train must have taken nearly all the night in crossing the burn. He shows that the rank and file of the army were much disheartened, and the lords had to tell them that, though often the overnight skirmishes might be favourable to one side, yet the main battle could be won by the other. The *Vita* says:

There was no rest or sleep, for men expected the Scots to make a night attack.

Gray:

> They had lost countenance and had been much upset by the events of the day.

The Lanercost chronicler:

> Thus fear fell upon the English, and the Scots were encouraged.

Nervousness was natural enough under such conditions. Yet we hear much next day of English pride and confidence, and one suspects that the talk about disheartening has been overdone in the light of next day's defeat. John of Trokelowe says, what is true doubtless of the best of men:

> They were bitter because of their repulse and vowed to be revenged on the morrow or die. . .they were hungry and had had no sleep.

Friar Baston's words are:

> While they thus boast with wine in the night revelling, They kill thee, Scotland, with vain words upbraiding. They sleep, they snore.

Baker, following this lead, tells of revelry and the drinking of healths. It is interesting to know that tongues were used to kill Bruce nearly six centuries before Kruger was heard of. But indeed are not accounts of the night before the battle usually more than a little coloured so that the fortunes of the battle itself may have a proper setting? The main point is that the English crossed the burn, and slept, or did not sleep, on the open ground towards Stirling.

CHAPTER 6

Monday, June 24th, 1314

The previous sections have shown that there is much to be said for Mr Mackenzie's theory that the main Battle of Bannockburn was fought on the Carse, not on the upland where it has been usually located. The evidence is very clear and strong that the English army crossed the Bannock after the double repulse of Bohun and Clifford, and encamped *outre Bannockburn* on the swampy ground where it meets the Forth. Clifford had fought on a plain field beneath the Kirk of St Ninian, some of his men had fled to Stirling Castle, and the garrison had come out to help the main army as it encamped; likewise on Monday King Edward fled to the castle and many with him; Barbour and Gray and the more nearly contemporary writers tell us this explicitly, and it is perfectly obvious that no fugitives could reach the castle after a fight on the upland with the victorious Scots in between.

If Clifford fought on the flat firm ground in the Carse, the same land was also possible for Monday's battle; there was space enough though not much to spare; near the Forth indeed were pools, but at the 50-foot contour and near to the foot of the upland the ground was known in the 18th century as the "dry lands," and this recalls the *arida terra* where Friar Baston puts the battle; *vide* the *Old Statistical Account of Scotland*, quoted by Mr Mackenzie. The word *campus*, used by two chroniclers, may indeed merely mean "battlefield," yet seems to point to a really flat stretch of ground, which suits the Carse and not the upland. These are general considerations based on good evidence. Then when we take the details of Monday's battle we have two military facts which make the matter certain.

Firstly, on the Sunday Bruce with the rear, his brother Edward supporting him, repulsed Bohun and the English van; Moray with the

Scottish van, supported by Douglas, routed Clifford. These were the rear and van of the army in retreat. Therefore Bruce was nearest to the English line of attack by the high road, and Moray was furthest off until Clifford rode round. But in Monday's battle Edward Bruce came first into action, then Moray on his flank, then Douglas on Moray's flank, while the King was in the rear of them all. This is from Barbour, who writes clearly and circumstantially, while no English chronicler gives any such close details. If Barbour is right and if Monday's fight was on the upland, then Bruce acted in an incomprehensible manner; he drew up his four brigades in a new position, made them cross each other, and generally ran a risk of clubbing his army and involving it in confusion, a risk such as no able tactician would ever run.

But if Barbour is right and the fight was in the Carse, what happened was that the Scots simply faced to their left, and each brigade in its own place came into action and there was no crossing. Thus Edward Bruce was now on the right flank, Moray in the centre, Douglas on the left, all *en échelon* by the right, and the king was now furthest from the enemy and in reserve. In fact Barbour has pointed out the Carse as the battlefield, and the Carse justifies both Barbour as an historian and Bruce as the able tactician that we always have believed him to have been.

Secondly, our best authorities indicate that the upland was wooded, it may be thickly wooded, by the New Park. The Scottish Army was at first hidden. The English van on Sunday did not expect to find the whole of the army so near them, and after Bohun's death retreated hastily as not only Bruce's rear brigade but also Edward Bruce's supporting brigade debouched from the wood. Again, on the Monday morning early the Scots debouched from the wood; and the English van attacked impetuously because the battle was forced on them, and the nine other brigades of horse came on behind and to a side in a disorderly mob. Now is it possible to imagine that, with the Bannock between, there was any need to accept battle so hastily, the rear being quite open? But let us grant, though it is against the evidence, that the English attack was hurried on by mere pride and over-confidence.

They had to cross the burn, and Sir Evelyn Wood, who examined the ground with a soldier's eye, has pointed out that they could only cross at three places and on a narrow front at each place, for to right and left the banks were too steep for the horses, and in front were swamps at intervals where the banks were low; we argued previously that Mr Mackenzie must be wrong in denying the existence of Milton Bog and Halbert Bog. They would have crossed very slowly, made some attempt to reform on the north bank, and ascended the slope to get within distance to charge and to put their lumbering horses into a canter. Meanwhile Bruce was looking on. If he was the able tactician he would have tumbled them all into the bed of the burn long ago. Or, if he had deliberately waited for all the English mounted men to be across so that he might lure them all to destruction, where was the open ground necessary for a charge of 2000 horses? Or, if the New Park did not cover most of the upland and if there was sufficient space, what are we to think of the chroniclers who make so prominent a feature of the wood?

In fact, if we are obsessed by the idea that the battle took place on the upland, difficulties meet us on every side, and thus we see how no two modern historians give the same account of the fighting. The most sane account is Sir Evelyn's, and it must stand if we accept the upland; it explains how the thing was done on the conditions of the site, but goes against the evidence. But no sooner do we shift the scene to the Carse than every condition is satisfied, as Mr Mackenzie alone has had the wit to see. The Scots debouched in their three brigades en echelon, advanced on the flat, forced the English to come on because they had caught them in the loop of the Forth and the Bannock, and continued to advance to the attack, merely halting to present a steady front at the moment of the English cavalry's disorderly charge. There were both time and space for the manoeuvres described, and yet neither time nor space for the English to array their lines properly. Therefore again we can say that Barbour indicates the Carse as the battlefield, and the Carse justifies both Barbour as an historian and Bruce as a tactician.

Let us next take the English chroniclers so that we can see where they corroborate or supplement Barbour. Various problems will be suggested, and then we shall be able to make a consistent account of the battle. Only let us remember that no general statement need be taken too literally, even if the evidence of an eyewitness is quoted. Any man only sees a part of a battle, and a chronicler may soon make a mistake if he infers too much from a statement which has to be conditioned by other circumstances of the battle. And first once more we place Sir Thomas Gray because he was a soldier, and his father was, since Clifford's defeat, a prisoner in Bruce's hands. Barbour says that Bruce had overnight held an informal council of war, had asked if his lords were ready to fight, and had been assured that they were. Gray's opening statement is quite compatible with Barbour's.

The Scots in the wood thought they had done well enough this day, and *were on the point of breaking camp* and retiring by night to the stronger country of the Lennox, when Alexander Seton, who had come with the army in the allegiance of the King of England, came secretly to Bruce in the wood, and said: 'Sire, now is the time, if ever, to think of re-conquering Scotland; the English have lost heart and are discouraged, and expect nothing but a sudden open attack.' So he told him of their condition, and declared, upon his head and under pain of being hung and drawn, that *if he would charge upon them in the morning he would defeat them easily* without loss to himself. Excited by this information the Scots made ready to fight, and at sunrise they *debouched from the wood in three battles on foot*, and marched stiffly upon the English, who had remained under arms all night with their horses bridled, and *who now mounted* in great haste; they were not accustomed to dismount to fight on foot, whereas the Scots had followed the example of the Flemings who had previously at Courtrai routed on foot the power of France.

The Scots came on in a line in the schiltrom formation, and charged upon the brigades of *the English, who were crowded together* and could not force their way towards them, so much were *their horses speared through the bowels*. (Here it is safe to adopt the punctuation of Sir Herbert Maxwell's translation; otherwise there is no sense in the passage.) *The rearmost English fell back upon the channel of the Bannockburn*, tripping over each other. Their brigades thrown into confusion by the thrusts of the spears upon the horses commenced to fly. Those who were appointed to ride at the king's bridle perceived the mischief, and *drew the king out of the battle towards the castle* much against his will. As the Scots on foot laid hold of the housing of the king's charger to stop him, he struck out so vigorously with his mace that he felled every man that he touched. The famous knight Sir Giles Argentine said, 'Sire, your rein was entrusted to me; there is the castle where your body will be safe. I am not accustomed to fly, and I am not going to begin now.' So he spurred into the thick of the fight and was killed. The king, mounted on a fresh horse, rode round the Torwood to Lowness, and so to Dunbar, thence by sea to Berwick.

Suggested site of Moray's battle on June 23rd and of the main battle on June 24th.

St Ninian's Kirk and the flat ground.

Next in value we place the *Chronicle of Lanercost*, because one fact at least, and from it presumably the whole account, comes from an eye-witness. It is a very minor matter that here the Scots are said to be in two brigades abreast, while Barbour makes them advance in three *en échelon* before they came abreast.

The next day either side made ready for battle. *The English archers went ahead of the main battle* and met the Scots' archers, and on either side some were slain and wounded, but the English soon routed the others. But when the two armies came close together, all the Scots knelt down to repeat the Lord's Prayer and commended themselves to God; *then they advanced boldly upon the English.* Their army was so arrayed that two brigades preceded the third, these two marching abreast, and in the third in the rear was Bruce. *When the shock of battle came and the great horses of the English dashed upon the Scottish spears as upon a dense forest,* there arose a great and horrible din from the broken lances and the wounded horses, and so for a time they stood locked together. But *the English who were coming up from the rear could not reach the Scots, because their own front line was in the way,* nor could they help them, and nothing remained but to think of flight. *This I heard from a trustworthy eyewitness.*

And this misfortune also befell the English; before the battle they had had to cross *a great ditch up which the tide comes from the sea, called the Bannokeburne, and, when in their confusion they tried to retreat, many in the press fell into it,* and some escaped with difficulty, while others were never able to extricate themselves; this Bannokeburne was on Englishmen's tongues for many years to come. 'Forth absorbed many well equipped with horses and arms, and Bannock mud many whose very names we know not' (this is a quotation from some poem.) The king with many others fled to Dunbar, led by a Scot who knew the country. Those who were slow in flight were slain by the fiercely pursuing Scots, but these had bravely formed themselves into a body and reached England safely.

The *Vita Edwardi Secundi* rather wastes time on the fate of Gloucester, and is badly wrong in giving the command to Douglas in place of Edward Bruce and in putting the strength of the Scots at 40,000. But it gives a picture of an English partisan's thoughts on the battle.

In the morning it was known that *the Scots were ready for battle* in great numbers. The older and more experienced advised that the battle should be put off to the morrow, because of the feast-day and of the *weariness of the army*. The younger men called this good advice cowardice. Gloucester was in favour of the delay, but the king hotly accused him of treachery. Meanwhile Bruce arrayed his men, and fed and inspirited them; and *when he saw that the English lines had come out on to the plain, he led his out of the wood*. They were 40,000 strong and in three brigades, all on foot, and all wearing light but sword-proof armour, axe at side and spear in hand. They marched in close order, and not easily could such an array be broken. When the armies came to the point of meeting, *James Douglas, who commanded the first brigade of Scots, sharply attacked Gloucester's line*. The earl withstood him manfully, and once and again broke into the wedge, and would have been victorious if his men had been faithful. But, as the Scots charged home, his horse was killed and he fell.

Unsupported and weighed down he could not rise, and of his whole contingent of 500 men-at-arms whom he brought to the war at his own expense hardly a man but himself was killed . . . *Some said that Gloucester was killed because of his own rashness. For there was rivalry between himself and Hereford, and each claimed the right to lead the van*, so that when the Scots came on quickly he dashed forward to have the glory, and thus was unsupported and killed. Twenty men could have rescued him, but out of 500 not one was found. Giles of Argentine tried to succour him, but could not; he did what he could and died with him. Those with the king saw the earl's line broken, and said that it was dangerous to remain there and the king should retire. So *he left the plain and hastened to the castle*. When his standard was seen in retreat the whole army scattered.

Over 200 knights neither drew sword nor struck a blow. O famous nation, invincible in days of old, you who used to conquer on horseback, why fly before infantry? You won at Berwick and Dunbar and Falkirk, and now you turn your backs to Scots on foot. . .Whilst our men were in flight following the king, *a great ditch engulfed many* and a great number died in it. The king reached the castle and expected to have refuge there, but was repulsed as if he were an enemy; the bridge was up and the gate closed. The governor has been accused of treason, and yet he was seen that day in arms for the king. I neither hold him guiltless nor accuse him, but confess that it was God's doing that the king did not enter the castle, for he could not but have been taken prisoner. Our men fled unarmed, and the Scots pursued for 50 miles. The countrymen, who had pretended to be peaceable, now slew the English or captured them to win the reward proclaimed by Bruce. Especially were the Scots anxious to take the magnates for their ransom.

Hereford, and over 500 who were thought to be dead, were afterwards ransomed. But most of the Scots turned to plunder the camp, for otherwise, if they had all been keen in the pursuit, few English would have escaped to Berwick. *I have never heard of such an army having been so suddenly routed by infantry, except when the flower of France fell before the Flemings at Courtrai.* Pride was the reason, and jealousy of any of higher rank, and love of wealth and plunder. It is thus that noble families die out, or inheritance passes to women.

The chronicle of Geoffrey Baker of Swinbroke is of value for the one definite statement that the English archers were useless in the rear. He clearly misunderstood what he was told about the pits, the sleepless night, the sun flashing on the armour.

To Stirling the king brought his forces with all the pomp usual *at that date when the chivalry of England still fought on horseback,* with curvetting chargers and flashing armour, and when men in their arrogant rashness were so confident that, in addition to the necessary equipment of horses and arms and provisions, they brought gold and silver vessels such as are used at the banquets of the mighty of the earth in days of peace. Men of that day had never seen such an overweening array of chivalry, as that poor Carmelite, friar Baston, in his poem on the campaign, at which he was present and was taken prisoner by the Scots, bewailed bitterly. That night you might have seen the English— not angels—*drenching themselves with wine and drinking healths,* while the Scots kept watch and fasted.

Next morning the Scots chose a fine position, and dug ditches three feet deep and three wide along the whole of their front from right to left, covering them over with intertwined branches, that is to say, hurdles, screened by grass, across which indeed infantry might pass if they knew the trick, but which could not bear the weight of cavalry. None of the Scots were allowed to mount their horses, and arrayed in brigades as usual they stood in a closely formed line behind the aforesaid cannily, I will not say deceitfully, constructed ditch. *As the English moved from the west the rising sun shone on their gilded shields and helmets.* Such a general as Alexander would have preferred to try conclusions on some other ground or other day, or at least would have waited till midday when the sun would have been on their right. But the impetuous and headstrong obstinacy of the English preferred death to delay.

In the front line were the cavalry with their heavy chargers, unaware of the concealed ditch; *in the second were the infantry, including the archers* who were kept ready for the enemy's flight; in the rear the king, with the bishops and other clerics, amongst them that foolish knight, Hugh the Spenser. *The front line of cavalry charged, and as the horses' legs were caught in the ditch through the hurdles, down fell the men* and died before the enemy could strike; and at their fall on came the enemy, slaughtering and taking prisoners, and sparing only the rich for ransom. There died Gilbert, Earl of Gloucester, whom the Scots would willingly have saved for ransom, if they had recognised him, but he was not wearing his coat-armour. *Many were killed by the archers of their own army, who were not placed in a suitable position, but stood behind the men-at-arms, whereas at the present day the custom is to post them on the flanks.* When they saw the Scots charging fiercely on the horsemen who had fallen at the ditch, some of them shot their arrows high in the air to fall feebly on the enemy's helmets, some shot ahead and hit a few Scots in the chest, and many English in the back. So all yesterday's pomp came to naught.

Three short extracts from minor English chroniclers are useful for one or another detail. Abbot Burton of Meaux, writing from earlier material, represents the current ideas of a later generation. The other two are all but contemporary.

The *Meaux Chronicle*:

So the English and Scots met on the *plain of Bannock* near Stirling, the English very proud and confident in their strength and numbers, the Scots after confession and communion calling on God alone as their protector. The armies being arrayed against each other, the *Scots put forward their foot in the front line, and the English their horse,* and at the first onset fortune gave victory to the Scots, and the English turned their backs and were slain . . .because iron spikes had been placed in hollows under the ground so that both horse and foot might trip . . .Edmund de Mauley, the king's *seneschal*, in his flight was intercepted by the water and drowned.

John of Trokelowe, a monk of St Albans:

The next day each army made ready for battle, and about the third hour they were drawn up in formidable array . . . *The English leaders put in their first line their infantry, archers and spearmen*; their cavalry, centre and wings, they drew up behind. . .*The Scots*, inspirited by the speeches of their leaders, resolutely *awaited the attack*; they were all on foot; picked men they were, enthusiastic, armed with keen axes and other weapons, and with their shields closely locked in front of them they *formed an impenetrable phalanx* . . .The cause of the disaster I do not know, unless it was that the English were too impetuous and disorderly; they were tired and weak, both men and horses, because of their excessive haste, and they were hungry and had had no sleep. Also the Scots, knowing the ground, which the English did not, *attacked sooner than was expected* (maturius) in dense battle array.

Gesta Edwardi de Carnarvan, by a canon of Bridlington:

The English did not fight in regular order but disconnectedly, in such a way that no one could support another . . .The king went to the castle of Stirling and there sought refuge. But Sir Alexander de Mowbray, knowing that his provisions could not suffice for himself and his garrison, and fearing that Bruce after his victory would come and attack the castle, refused to allow his lord, the King of England, to run such a risk, and therefore *would not open the castle to him*.

The name Alexander is wrong, but the statement confirms very strongly the king's flight to the castle.

Now we can put together the various statements. And first as to the pits, we can only repeat that Baker and Abbot Burton had two facts before them, the digging of pits as described by Baston, and the tripping of the English cavalry in the bed of the burn when they broke and fled; these two facts they confused together. But Barbour, better informed, located the pits on either side of the high road which crossed the burn and climbed up to the entry into the wood; but he is entirely silent about pits on the Monday, for the plain fact is that the battle was in the Carse where none were dug. All the other chroniclers, Barbour himself included, tell us of a straight charge of English horse on the Scottish pikes without any hint of pits or tripping. But the English tripped in their flight as they were driven into the Bannock.

That the Scots attacked and forced on a battle is beyond doubt. Once decided not to retreat to the stronger country of the Lennox, Bruce was wise to attack. Whether disheartened or over-confident, the English were but an armed mob. Sunday had proved that. If only he could trust his men to be steady the game was in his hands, and his men were steady after many years of hard work and adventurous deeds against the castles of Scotland and their English garrisons. In the meanwhile the English barons had only been wrangling about their rights at home against Edward II. Aymer de Valence, Beaumont, Clifford, Despenser, and many others, had already fought and had lost many of their horses at Falkirk; they knew that pikes could repulse cavalry, but were powerless against well-posted archers, and that on the Sunday Moray had beaten two of them; yet they had no notion of an orderly attack. It was no light task for pikemen to advance in good order even against a mob of horse. Llewelyn's Welsh and Wallace's rings of Scots at Falkirk could stand against horse, but Bruce's superiority over them was that he could make his men move forward in lines without losing their formation, though encumbered with their long pikes, like the Macedonians of old and the Swiss of the middle ages.

It was traditional after Bannockburn for the Scots to move to the attack, and they did so at Halidon Hill and at Neville's Cross where they were beaten. But though he attacked, he must have trained his men to halt to receive cavalry a few moments before the impact came; technically he was on the offensive so as to bring the English nobles to make their impetuous charge, but for the moment each body of pikemen was on the defensive. Even so Henry V at Agincourt advanced, galled the French and made them deliver their countercharge, and stood steady to receive it. There is no way otherwise of understanding the nature of the shock of the mailed English horse and horsemen, the din of the splintered spears, the squeals of the speared animals, etc.; see Gray and the *Lanercost Chronicle* as above.

The Scots moved *en échelon* by the right. Edward Bruce led, and Gloucester with the van made the countercharge upon him; we may suppose that the bend of the Bannock protected the outer flank, which is ever the weak point of a solid line of infantry. The result is clear. The *Vita* implies that the earl was ahead of his men and badly supported, but that the battle was fierce and long is allowed even by Barbour. The English tried to break in and failed, and the Scots, the full force of the charge once expended, pushed on slowly and relentlessly, stabbing the horses and disembowelling them; slowly it must have been, for the dead horses had to be passed cautiously so that the ranks should not be broken.

Meanwhile Moray's men had moved up on Edward Bruce's left till they were abreast, Douglas did the same on Moray's left; for Barbour is clearly describing the events in order of time. Both received the mob of nine other brigades of English horse. Who counted nine does not appear, and among the English chroniclers not one gives that number. It is quite immaterial. Medieval armies had a right or van, main, left or rear, and reserve corps; the sub-division of these was rare. But in any case the nine were massed, says Barbour, into one schiltrom, one mob of shields. There was no effort to manoeuvre, no time to form squadrons for alternate attack, no space to do it in, no wish and no ability to do aught else than charge straight ahead. The eye-witness who informed the Lanercost chronicler tells the same tale as Barbour and Gray.

Meanwhile, we ask, where were the English archers? The Lanercost chronicler and Trokelowe put them in the first line; Baker puts them in the rear; Gray and the *Vita* and Abbot Burton say nothing about them, and consider the battle to have been an affair of horse on one side and foot on the other. May not they all be right, each from his own point of view? We have just read how Barbour described the battle from the Scottish right flank towards the left, as Edward Bruce, Moray, and Douglas came in turn into action. We are next told, after Douglas has struck in, how "the English archers shot so fast that it had been hard to Scottish men." Clearly they were shooting on the extreme Scottish left. We are quite justified in saying that the English king did throw out a skirmishing line of archers, that probably they did not intervene between Edward Bruce and Gloucester, but that, after scattering for a time the Scottish archer skirmishers, they gradually drew to their right, *i.e.* northwards, so as to allow those nine brigades of horse to charge Moray and Douglas, and that then they were shooting into Douglas' left flank. But Bruce was ready for them.

There was no thought-out plan of the relative positions of cavalry and archers; Halidon Hill and Crécy were in the future, and were indeed victories of dismounted cavalry and archers combined for the very reason that the lesson of Bannockburn was taken to heart. Bruce saw well enough that the archers could only come into play on the flank if the cavalry were to attack straight ahead. He had his marshal, Robert Keith, ready in the wood, with 500 horsemen "armed well in steel that on light horse were horsed well." He launched them at the critical moment, and they cut up the archer wing. Horsemen, once in among foot that they have surprised, are irresistible.

Given a loose order so that as many archers as possible may shoot at once, obviously they cover a great deal of ground. A thousand, perhaps two thousand of them, were in action and were routed by Keith; there was no room for more. The rest, 10,000 or more or less—who can possibly know? but at least we may be absolutely certain that there were not 30,000—must have been in the rear and useless. Very probably many of them did shoot some of the English cavalry in the back, or shot without aim into the air so that the arrows fell and did no harm to the helmets of the Scots. Baker writes this as one who knew that at Crécy the archers were in hollow wedges supported by dismounted knights on a thought-out plan, whereas the whole story of Edward II shows want of forethought. Are we to reject Baker's judgment on the one thing that he knew, the evolution of archery and the formation of the archers in the battle, just because he writes nonsense about the pits and sun in the eyes of the English?

Common sense shows that Gray and others thought only of the cavalry charge, the Lanercost man thought most of the cavalry but knew that there was an archer line of skirmishers, and Baker neglecting these skirmishers insisted on the bulk of the archers being out of action in the rear. Barbour has enabled us to understand where the comparatively small number of archers did come into action and at what moment of the battle. He also adds that the Scottish archers now came into action and contributed to the confusion of the English.

The end of the battle is easy to narrate. Bruce, seeing the English horsemen powerless and the archers routed, thought the moment ready to put in his reserve which was assembled "on a side"; whether this was on Edward Bruce's right or on Douglas' left does not appear. "Their foes were rushed," yet they still fought on. All four brigades of Scots pressed on, and the Scottish archers, beaten off by the English archers at the first onset, now contributed to the final rout. The last episode, the charge of the camp-followers—who are not termed "gillies" by Barbour, but "yhemen swanys and poueraill," *i.e.* yeomen and swains and poor men—has been exaggerated. The English would have broken and fled, if the charge had not taken place. We finish by acknowledging that Barbour does justice to the fighting qualities of the English, King Edward included, and indicates that it was a long and hard battle.

A glance at the passages given above will satisfy any serious student of history that Edward II did escape from the field to the castle. That Mowbray was wise in refusing to admit him is beyond doubt. Certain capture would have resulted. He fled beneath the castle, round by the "Round Table," and ultimately to Linlithgow, thence to Dunbar, thence to Berwick by boat. He was not a coward, and had fought in the battle fiercely with his mace. Other Englishmen fled as best they could, if once they escaped from drowning in the Forth and Bannock. The Scots slew very many, but the temptation to pause and plunder the camp was great. Also their hope of making money by ransom is indicated by more than one chronicler. The Earl of Hereford was captured after escaping to Bothwell Castle on the Clyde. Aymer of Valence alone of the great men got clear away.

The most complete list of the slain is given in the *Annates Londinienses,* and includes Gloucester, Clifford, Tibetot, William and Anselm Marshal, Bohun, Edmund Mauley the Seneschal of the Household, Edmund and John Comyn, Dayncourt, in all 37 nobles and knights. Several of the names can be identified as those of men in Gloucester's and Hereford's retinues who had letters of protection for the campaign. A certain amount of interest is attached to the fate of Giles of Argentine, who rode at his king's rein and sacrificed himself to let the king escape; the *Vita* makes out that he died in trying to save Gloucester, but the author has Gloucester on the brain. Giles was one of those landed proprietors of comparatively humble position who rose as fighting men to some eminence, like John Chandos and Nigel Loring, the close comrades of the Black Prince a generation later. He had served at Falkirk as a squire in the retinue of Hugh Despenser, and as a knight in 1310 in the feudal contingent of Piers Gaveston, Earl of Cornwall. He was famed as a Crusader, but never had a chance of showing himself to be a tactician as well as a mere fighter.

One may, indeed, find fault with Barbour because he has made people think too much of the unimportant things, the digging of the pots, the deaths of Bohun and Argentine, the charge of the camp-followers, which things the thoughtless love to read, and think to be of more importance than the tactics. Yet he has shown us the real cause of the victory, namely the steadiness of the pikemen, their ability to advance in good order, and the clever handling of the whole army of foot and light horse by a great tactician.

From above Foot o' Green, looking towards the English encampment on the night of the 23rd

CHAPTER 7

After Bannockburn

After Bannockburn, Bruce raided the Border Counties every year and spread terror far and wide. His purpose was not to fight a pitched battle, but to devastate and to levy black-mail. The account which is given to us of the raid in 1327, conducted by James Douglas when Bruce himself was on his deathbed, is probably typical of many similar raids; it is given to us by Jehan le Bel, a Hainaulter who had come to England in the train of John of Hainault, uncle of Philippa the future Queen of England, from whom Froissart drew his account of many of the events of the early part of Edward III's reign. The Scots were all mounted on ponies, and carried, besides their light armour and weapons, bags of oatmeal and gridirons from which they made girdle cakes, but otherwise they subsisted upon the cattle that they captured. They were always able to keep a little distance ahead of the heavier cavalry of the English and Hainaulters, so that the bones of the pursuers ached as they continued to ride day after day, ever clothed in their iron armour and unable to catch their nimble foes. But this account is of the first year of Edward III and at least shows that the English court made an effort to save the Northern Counties; Edward II himself between 1314 and the end of his reign did very little indeed, being ever troubled by the continued insubordination of Lancaster and Hereford and their party.

In Cumberland and Westmoreland, the English having to defend themselves as best they could, there came to the front Andrew de Harcla: we know that in 1310 he was a knight in the retinue of John Cromwell, the husband of a great Westmoreland heiress, and from 1312 onwards he was custodian of the town and castle of Carlisle. In 1314 after Bannockburn, and again in 1315, he raised considerable forces to check the raiding Scots, besides defending Carlisle successfully, but in 1316 he was prisoner in Bruce's hands, and was afterwards ransomed. The special point of interest is that Andrew appears to have done most to raise a light cavalry that could move as quickly as the Scots themselves. In the regular armies of Edward I and Edward II we hardly ever find any mention of light cavalry except when a few hobelars were brought over from Ireland. In Andrew's force in garrison in Carlisle in 1314 we find three knights, 50 men-at-arms, 30 hobelars, and 100 archers, but in 1319 he took to the army which was raised to try to recapture Berwick 980 foot and 380 hobelars without any heavy cavalry at all. It would seem that these men were arrayed and equipped in imitation of the light Irish cavalry, and that the name hobelar was applied to them from the Irish.

In 1322 the contest between King Edward and Lancaster came to a crisis; Andrew came down from Westmoreland to help his king, and took up a position to contest the passage of the River Ure at Boroughbridge against Lancaster and his ally Hereford. He dismounted his horsemen, most of them presumably hobelars, to defend, in a solid body of spears, both the bridge and ford "in the Scottish manner," *i.e.* in a schiltrom, and on the flanks of each schiltrom he arrayed his archers. Hereford was killed at the bridge, and Lancaster was repulsed at the ford and surrendered next day.

In a similar manner Sir Thomas Gray, who had been ransomed since Bannockburn, and who was commissioned by Edward II in 1322 to be custodian of Norham Castle—the Bishop of Durham's garrison at Norham was thought to be too weak, and therefore the king claimed his right to send a custodian of his own choosing— fought in the Scottish manner with his spearmen in a schiltrom on foot; we have the description of his son, the author of the *Scalacronica*, of a sortie made by the garrison of Norham on foot, while a certain adventurous knight. Sir William Marmion, who had come thither to do some desperate feat of arms for love of his lady, charged recklessly ahead on horseback; Marmion was borne to earth, but Gray and his spearmen on foot came up in time to rescue him and beat off the Scots by spearing their horses; and then the women of the garrison brought up their horses for them to mount and pursue.

But when Edward II, hoping after Lancaster's death that he might be able to invade Scotland and reverse the verdict of Bannockburn, raised an army in 1322, he completely misunderstood the military needs of the time. Instead of raising hobelars whom he could dismount and convert into foot spearmen in battle, while they could

Stirling from the North: the reported site beyond, and the suggested site to the left of the rock.

move as quickly as the Scots before battle, he deliberately summoned from all the counties of England foot spearmen only, and these were not summoned with archers but instead of archers. The force of folly could no further go; such an army could only march very slowly, and as Bruce remained true to his principle of refusing pitched battle, the entire force, some 14,000 strong, half of them Welsh, half of them Englishmen toiled painfully over the moors, and starved, and a sadly reduced number returned home in a state of terrible disorder.

At last, in the early years of Edward III, somebody, we do not know who it was, saw that the only chance of victory that England had depended on the application of the tactics used by Harcla and Gray, that the employment of foot spearmen was useless unless they were mounted for marching, and unless they were supported by archers. In 1332, after the death of Bruce, Edward Balliol made a bid to conquer his father's throne, and was accompanied by some English adventurers. He invaded Scotland by sea and landed on the coast of Fife. On his way towards Perth he encountered a superior force of the Scots at Dupplin Moor. The heavy cavalry were dismounted and drawn up in the centre, and archers were posted on either wing; the Scots charged, of course on foot, and nearly broke the English centre, but the arrows from the two wings threw them into disorder and blinded them, and they collapsed. Next year King Edward III of England invaded Scotland as the open ally of Balliol, and laid siege to Berwick; the Scottish army appeared to save the town, for by treaty it was to be surrendered unless relieved by a given date.

The English were drawn up on the north side of Halidon Hill, barring the way against the relieving Scots. They were formed in three brigades and a reserve. The formation of Boroughbridge and of Dupplin Moor was adopted, but with a difference; each of the three brigades had a centre of dismounted cavalry, and each also had two wings of archers which sloped outwards towards the enemy; the result was that the right wing of the left brigade, and the left wing of the centre brigade formed a hollow wedge pointing at the enemy; and similarly the right wing of the centre and the left wing of the right. Later, after the Battle of Crécy, this hollow wedge of archers was called a *herse*, i.e. harrow[1].

The importance of the military reform which was so strikingly successful at the Battle of Halidon Hill comes from the fact that at last knights and archers were properly combined in action; for not only in

---

1. Mr Hereford George first proved that the *herse* was a hollow wedge.

all future battles was each brigade composed of knights and archers, but also the hollow wedges formed between the brigades connected the army as a whole. And whereas at Boroughbridge Harcla's army had probably but few men of high rank in it, and at Dupplin Moor a mere band of adventurers were fighting, now at Halidon Hill the king himself and several earls and high barons were present in person. Therefore, although Baker is not literally correct when he says that this was the first battle in which the English fought all on foot, it was at least the first battle on a large scale in which the tactics were adopted which became the normal English method of fighting, and led the way to Crécy and Agincourt.

Baker's account is as follows:

> The English Army was divided, part being told off to continue the siege, part to meet the Scots. Here the English Chivalry learnt from the Scots to reserve their horses for the pursuit of fugitives, and themselves to fight on foot, contrary to their fathers' practice. . .The two armies came together, and after a fierce resistance barely up to mid-day, the Scots having lost a great number of men and their three brigades rolled up into one, the King and his men mounted their horses and quickly pursued, slaying, capturing, and driving the enemy into ponds and swamps.

The Lanercost Chronicler says:

> The Scots of the first brigade were so wounded in the face and so blinded by the multitude of arrows as in the previous Battle of Gledenmoor (Dupplin Moor) that they were quite helpless and tried to turn away their faces. And as the English were formed like the Scots into three brigades Balliol being on the left of the three, the Scots swerved out of their original line of attack and fell upon him, but were soon routed, similarly the other two brigades were routed; then the English mounted in pursuit.

These are general descriptions which give the honour of the victory to the archers, backed as they were by the dismounted men-at-arms, and posted in their hollow wedges in such a way that their flanks could not be turned, so that the enemy was forced into making a frontal attack. The Chronicler of Bridlington is the authority who definitely states that the archers were posted on each wing of each brigade, and he adds that while the leading Scots brigade attacked Balliol on the left, and their second attacked the English centre, the third wheeled against the English right and held up just long enough to allow a picked body of 200 well-horsed Scots to charge round along the foot of Halidon Hill to carry the needed relief to Berwick; if these should reach the city walls a formal relief would be effected according to the ideas of the age. But King Edward also had a picked body of horse in readiness, which moving upon inner lines headed them off and drove them into the sea.

There was nothing rigid in the new tactics. It was not necessary to have always three brigades of dismounted knights abreast with four hollow wedges between them and on their flanks. This was the formation at Halidon Hill, where there was also a reserve; it was also the formation at Agincourt, where Henry V had no reserve because he had no men to spare. At Crécy, two brigades were roughly abreast, the Black Prince's and Northampton's, and the King's main body was in reserve at the top of the slope. Amongst the hedges and vineyards of Poitiers—or rather at the hamlet of Maupertuis some miles from Poitiers—the men were arrayed quite irregularly; at Auray there were three brigades each of 500 men-at-arms and 300 archers with a reserve.

In all the battles it is clear that the enemy, whether mounted or on foot, might be able to force their way between the storm of arrows which flew from the hollow wedges, and then they would instinctively swerve inwards from the wedges into the space in front of the dismounted men-at-arms, but then the arrows would be shot into their flanks, the men-at-arms in the background would hold them up, and the terrible slaughter that occurred would be due to the suffocation of the unfortunate men massed together and driven inwards against each other. The language used by chroniclers of Dupplin Moor and Neville's Cross and Agincourt might suit any one of the battles. Also if the English were fighting on ground especially chosen to suit their tactics they were always able to make a deadly countercharge.

There is yet one more military form to be noticed; we have hardly any documentary evidence about the campaign of Halidon Hill, we simply know that the archers were there, and that they were in considerable numbers; we also know from the Scottish roll of 1333 that all sorts and conditions of men had been impressed into the ranks, and pardons were given to criminals who had served there. But we do not know if the horse-archer had yet been invented. The first occasion

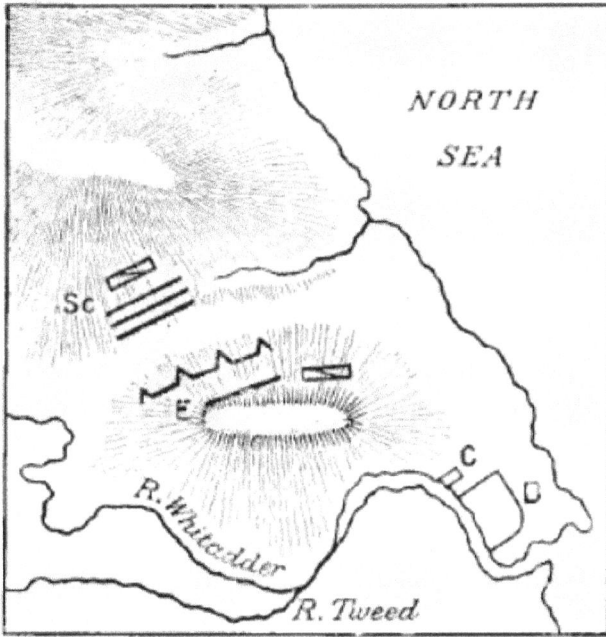

BATTLE-PLAN OF HALIDON HILL.

HALIDON HILL FROM BERWICK.

when we know that the bulk of the archers in a particular army were mounted was when the Earls of Salisbury and Gloucester laid siege to Dunbar 1337-8. At this siege all the archers were mounted; Yorkshire supplied 400, Northamptonshire 140, Lancashire 130, Lincolnshire 120, Norfolk 114, Nottinghamshire 100, Derbyshire 100, and other counties smaller numbers; but the whole of England was represented, except the counties of the south and southwest coast from Sussex round to Somerset: Kent sent 96, and even Rutlandshire 40. The total came to just over 1920 men, while Wales supplied 466 foot archers.

The next development was that barons and bannerets who raised soldiers for the king by contract levied almost equal numbers of heavy armed cavalry and horse-archers. At the siege of Calais, in the month before the town fell, when Edward III had received large reinforcements in anticipation of the French attack, there were present about 1000 knights, 4000 men-at-arms, and 5000 horse-archers, while the foot archers came to 15,000, and the Welsh contingent was 4400. The same year to patrol the borders of Scotland against the Scots the north-country English lords had out 480 heavy cavalry and 2800 horse-archers. Meanwhile the hobelar has almost disappeared from a normal English army; there were merely 500 hobelars present at the siege of Calais.

It is clear therefore that the defeat at Bannockburn made Englishmen think. The immediate effect we saw previously was that in Cumberland and Westmoreland self-defence showed the necessity of mounting men who were light-armed on ponies, so as to catch up with the swiftly moving Scottish raiders, who simply mocked the clumsy mailed knights on heavy horses. Edward II, we saw, was stupid enough to consider the defeat at Bannockburn due to the deficiency of the archers, and put in their place heavy spear-armed infantry, who were worse than useless. Harcla first dismounted his hobelars for pitched battle. But who was the reformer who copied Harcla's method and beat the Scots at Dupplin Moor on a small scale, and at Halidon Hill on a large scale, who saw that the mounted archer would be more efficient than the hobelar, for he could ride as fast and then shoot on foot, we do not know.

Clearly the problem was to use the efficient bowman and at the same time to protect him from a sudden attack of cavalry from the flank. The problem was solved, and thus the northern counties, which had been paralysed by Bruce's raids, were able in 1346 to defend themselves without calling upon Edward III to send a man home from his encampment before Calais. In fact Scotland taught England to be warlike, and France suffered in consequence. The victories of the Hundred Years' War were certainly not beneficial to the English themselves; that they became proud and loved fighting for fighting's sake is only too apparent. But while we moralise upon the wickedness of war we can at least acknowledge that self-defence is a necessity.

Note. Since this book was in print I made a find in the Records Office which I am able to add to the last chapter. The pay-roll of part of the English army at Neville's Cross is extant, and tells us that in Lancashire were raised 960 horse-archers and 240 foot archers, and in Yorkshire 3200 horse-archers; but as the Lancashire men were paid up to October 17 and received in addition £20 *pro bono apparatu suo ultra vadia sua de dono regis,* and the Yorkshiremen were only paid up to October 16, the latter and bigger contingent was not up in time for the battle which was on the 17th. The roll moreover tells us that David Bruce was seriously wounded, for two barber-surgeons of York were paid to go to Bamborough, where he lay *sagitta vulneratus, ad dictam sagittam extrahendam.*

Further details will be published in the *Transactions* of the Royal Historical Society. Of course the north-country lords must have had out some heavy cavalry. Other horse-archers must have been supplied by the four counties nearer to the border, but serving in self-defence they would not be paid. The main interest of the roll is that mounted infantry in 1346-47 were raised as a matter of course. At this date the mounted archer had 4*d.* a day as his pay, his corporal or vintenar 6*d.*, and the foot archer 2*d.* as in the reigns of Edwards I and II, if they served in England; but the horse had 6*d.* and the foot 3*d.* when they served in France.

Also an article has appeared recently (April 1914) in the *Scottish Historical Review* by Sir Herbert Maxwell, in which he justifies, against Mr Mackenzie, his description of Bannockburn as fought on the traditional battlefield. In the first place I am now able to correct—and hasten to do so with an apology for a misconception—the assumption in my text that Sir Evelyn Wood was alone responsible for the battle-plan, which Sir Herbert gave in his *Bruce*, and which he now says that he had himself drawn up before Sir Evelyn's notes, given to him later, were found to confirm it. But Sir Herbert's article does not shake my belief in Mr Mackenzie. It is easy to find a mistake in this or that chronicle, to say that an eyewitness who is anonymous should not necessarily be believed, in fact to pick to pieces the evidence. My main argument in support of Mr Mackenzie is drawn from a general survey of the internal evidence; if we find Barbour's account consistent and intelligible, and if the English chroniclers' main facts fit in well with his, we are justified in following him.

Thus I feel that in trying to reconcile the apparently conflicting accounts of the share of the English archers in Monday's battle I am on the right lines, for each chronicler or his informant had something definite to tell of one aspect of the fight, and if the statements can be reconciled the presumption is that the general theory is more or less right. Minor mistakes as to the doings of Argentine or Bohun, Douglas or Clifford, can be corrected, when once one bases a general theory on all the chroniclers. Meanwhile Sir Herbert has not, as yet, explained how the way to Stirling was clear to the king and other English fugitives; he has not considered the question of the extent of the New Park which hid the Scots, or of the change in the Scottish line of battle. As for what he says about the difficulty that the English army would experience in making on Sunday evening a wide detour to an encampment in the Carse while Bruce was ready to pounce on the flank, I would answer that Bruce was then meditating retreat, and that Barbour may be fairly considered to indicate that the passage of the burn—which may have taken place a good way down, *i.e.* at the present town of Bannockburn—occupied most of the night.

Sir James Ramsay, I neglected to say in the text, made a battle-plan of the archers drawn up in hollow wedges at Agincourt[2] before Mr Hereford George wrote on this point. Also it is due to Sir James Ramsay more than to anyone else that the old belief in very large armies is now dying out. But he seems too quick to rush to the opposite extreme. I agree that the feudal levy of 1310 was very small indeed, but I submit that practically every baron that year sent to the muster the barest minimum of men on a very narrow interpretation of strict feudal duty. However in 1314 only some few barons sent their bare *debi-*

---

2. In his volumes on *Lancaster and York*.

tum servitium, and the others voluntarily served with retinues which, from the evidence of the letters of protection, were of considerable strength; and my contention is that the difference between a retinue raised under compulsion and a retinue raised voluntarily or even eagerly would be considerable.

Lastly, as Sir James Ramsay writes with such authority that many take his descriptions as *ipso facto* proved, I wish respectfully to protest against his assumption that Bruce drew up his men for battle always in rings; Wallace did at Falkirk, Moray did in Sunday's fight against Clifford, but if Bruce did so on Monday his men could not have advanced. The hollow ring is strictly defensive. But the Scots, as I contend that Mr Mackenzie rightly argues, attacked on the Monday, though they stood to receive the impact of the English cavalry; and the Scots charged at Dupplin Moor and Halidon Hill with Bannockburn's example in their minds. There is nothing to force us to believe that the schiltroms were always rings.

The Battle of Bannockburn

Contents

To Every True Scotsman,
Rich or Poor,
Whose Ancestors May Have Fought With
The Bruce at Bannockburn,
And Whose Heart Glows With Patriotism
As He Ponders
Over the Freedom and Independence Achieved
For Their Country by
The Warriors of Scotland
On That Memorable Battlefield,
This Volume
Is Respectfully Dedicated by
The Author.

Although our honoured patriots sleep in dust,
The glory they achieved we now enjoy;
Then let us venerate their very names,
And gaze upon the soil as hallowed ground
Whereon they fought and conquered!

CHAPTER 1

Preliminary Observations

In 1285, on the death of Alexander the Third, and even down to the decease of his grand-daughter, Margaret of Norway, in 1290, the people of Scotland were in the enjoyment of much comfort and prosperity. After that period, however, by the aggressive movements of Edward the First of England, they were subjected to a course of trial and suffering of the most severe kind, which lasted almost a quarter of a century. Her nobles and principal men unfortunately were more ready to promote their own personal interest than advance the independence of their country, hence they separated from each other, and the cause of patriotism suffered accordingly. Many arranged themselves on the side of England, while only a few proved true men, resolving to maintain the glory and honour of Scotland.

The middle classes and peasantry, ever subject to oppression from those above them, were levied time after time to form the ranks of defensive war, and when we consider the numerous conflicts in which they were engaged, and the exterminating tendency of these broils, it appears strange that such numbers still survived, on whose strength both Wallace and Bruce were able to contend with, and often to overcome, their more powerful enemies. The lands also, which in the time of David the First, from proper cultivation, produced excellent crops, were now neglected, and had it not been that sheep and cattle were still kept in those districts seldom visited by the English, that deer and other game were found in the wild uplands, and fish in the rivers and sea, many poor people must have died of hunger.[1]

---

1. The contest that ensued was of unexampled length and severity, and, in its sad course, the Scotch, notwithstanding their heroic resistance, and the victories they occasionally gained, had to endure every evil which could be inflicted by their proud and insolent neighbour.—Buckle, vol. iii.

About the period from 1290 to 1314 Scotland presented a very different aspect from what we behold at present. Nearly all its valleys, and large portions of its low-lying ground, were densely covered with trees and brushwood, which had grown up without any aid from the hand of man.[2] These forests, in many places, where the land consisted of mountain and dale, ascended far up the sides of the hills, affording shelter and sustenance to those wild beasts of chase which were common to the country.[3] The higher and more open ranges were often wild and barren, which, under attention, might have afforded food for sheep or cattle; but where these did not exist, the wide moors became waste land, dry and unproductive in summer, while throughout winter they were soaked in water.

Interspersed here and there were extensive morasses tufted with heather, but below, soft moss many feet deep formed swamps altogether impassable to man or beast. Green spots might be seen around villages, and at no great distance from towns, which had once been under the plough; but Nature was again resuming her sway, silently but surely, over the efforts of man, while many a fair field and broad acre, which we see pastured by thriving sheep and cattle, or waving with ripening grain in harvest, were covered then with gorse, bent, and heath, awaiting more peaceable times, that they might be turned to good account for the benefit and improvement of society.

In the brilliant pages of Macaulay, (volume 1), we have a striking picture of the badness of the highways in England during the reign of Charles the Second, but in Scotland, at the commencement of the fourteenth century, very few roads intersected the country, and these, from their imperfect state, could hardly be accounted public ways, save one or two direct lines of transit which had been formed eleven hundred years before by the Romans. When the soil over which any of these had been made was soft or liable to be washed away by rain, they were only tracks whereon a man might travel on horseback, but altogether unfit for carriages save in the time of summer. Others of less length might be found between inland towns, and, occasionally, from these to places on the seashore, for the purposes of import or export, and such lines had been constructed principally by the order of monks of several establishments, who, to their credit be it said, in

---

2. There is every sort of proof that every district of Caledonia, as the name implies, was anciently covered with woods.—Chalmers, vol i.

3. The face of the country was covered by immense forests, chiefly of oak.—Tytler, vol ii.

early times were ever ready to promote the welfare of the people.

The lands and houses they possessed were let to tenants—a part of the rent only to be paid in money, and the rest in manual service; and these landlords clearly perceived the advantage of having access to the nearest ports, whereby they might sell what produce they could spare, and purchase other commodities of which they were in want. The towns were small, few, and thinly populated, the inhabitants being chiefly dealers in small wares, weavers, shoemakers, joiners, and smiths, although the scope of the latter trades was very limited, because, from a very early date down to the beginning of the fifteenth century, not only rustic implements employed in agriculture, but armour, spears, bows, and arrows, were imported from Flanders.[4] Throughout the period of which we intend to treat, cultivation of the ground was overlooked, corn crops were neither sown nor reaped,[5] all other domestic pursuits were neglected, while the strength and genius of the male population were by circumstances directed to one object only, and that was war.

We may therefore perceive that much attention was paid to the equipment of men for the field, and by the intercourse Scotland maintained with the Continent, Robert Bruce and his knights were arrayed after the most approved fashion.[6] By that monarch's seal, he appears mounted on horseback, his arms and legs are covered with linked mail, the spur of the nearest being plainly visible. His helmet is cylindrical, with openings something like the letter T, and pierced also with square holes, while the top is adorned with a crown, on which are three ornamental crosses, or *fleurs-de-lis*, between each of which is a point, or precious stone. His body-armour, which consisted probably of steel plate, is covered by the surcoat, on which is shown the Scottish lion, and the same noble animal is depicted on the housings both on the shoulder and the hind-quarter of his horse. The like emblem figures within the double tressure on his shield, which is borne on his

---

4. Buckle, vol. iii.—In 1425 'it is ordaned be the King and the Parliament, that all merchands of the realm, passand over sea for merchandice, bring hame, as he male gudly thoile, after the quantity of his merchandice, harnes and armoures, with epeares, schaftes, bowes, and staues. And that be done be ilk ane of them als oft as it happenis them to passe ouer sea in merchandice.'—*Scots Acts*, fol. 7.

5. The labourers either fled or were murdered, and there being no one to till the ground, some of the fairest parts of Scotland were turned into a wilderness, overgrown with briars and thickets.—Buckle, vol. iii.

6. The knight and noble, before the days of Robert Bruce, rode armed in mail, always of foreign manufacture, from Flanders or Italy.— *Innes.*

left arm, and the ends of the cross-bar of his sword are turned slightly upwards from the right hand which grasps it. His brother, Sir Edward Bruce, his nephew, Thomas Randolph Earl of Moray, young Walter the High Steward, and James Douglas, all wore defensive armour, including shields, after the same manner.

The knights and horse-soldiers were similarly equipped, and the offensive weapons of the whole were each a long lance, a battle-axe slung from the shoulder, a sword on the left, and a long knife or dagger on the right side. The armour of the foot-soldiers were each a skull-cap of iron, first brought into use by their countryman Michael Scott, of wizard fame, (domestic astrologer of Emperor Frederick II.), a hanketon or garment of leather, on which folds of cloth were quilted, reaching from the neck to below the knee, and covering the arms so as to ward off either thrust or blow. They were armed nearly in the same way as the horsemen, having each a target or shield made of light but tough material, such as skin, a pike or spear[7] eighteen feet in length, a battle-axe, also a sword and a strong knife for use in close combat.

The archers were not so well defended as the spearmen, for they were without shields, but in addition to the bow and ample sheaf of arrows, they had the sword, the dagger, and battleaxe, which was used with deadly effect upon knights and men-at-arms when thrown to the ground. Scotland had few mounted warriors, and these rode small horses, consequently her defenders were unable to cope with the chivalry of England, troops of whom were covered, horse and man, in complete mail. Each Scottish knight was attended by two, three, or more squires, who waited upon him, held his horse, enabled him to mount, and bore such portions of his equipment as he might require in battle."

The man-at-arms likewise had his sergeants to perform the same round of duties. Accordingly, a regular army of foot and horse in England or Scotland, whether stationary or on the march, was always accompanied by a promiscuous multitude of male and female followers, amounting in number to two-thirds or more of the martial men, and

---

7. The Scotch spear was six elns long, or five elns 'before the burr,' 'of a clyft,' that is of one piece, a length which, at least in later times, obliged the spear-staves to be drawn from foreign countries, A fully-armed Scotch soldier had one of these formidable pikes, an axe, with a knife for finishing the work which these might leave imperfect, and a large shield of hide, 'to resist the shot of England.'—*Notes* to *The Brus*, by Innes. The burr was a broad iron ring fixed on the tilting lance behind the handle. It is shown in a cut in Guillim. See also Hall's *Henry IV.*, fol, xii., and Middleton, vol. ii.

these gave assistance to the regular soldiers in seeking water, preparing food, washing, repairing clothes and harness, and cleaning weapons and armour of every description."

Before this period the arrangement of an army in battle-array was most simple. In the early ages, and down to the fifteenth century, to lead the right wing was always considered as the chief post of honour. This arose from the front lines bearing the shield on the left arm, consequently that side was best defended, and the assailing troops had thereby the least chance of vanquishing their opponents. But towards the fourteenth century the preparation for battle, both in England and Scotland, exhibited no great amount of either skill or genius.[8] The infantry on either side was usually placed in several bodies, each under its respective leader, and between these, or near the wings, were the companies of archers, often divided, but when the ground was favourable keeping together, that their shafts might tell with more deadly effect on any particular quarter of the enemy.

Much importance, however, was now placed on the English cavalry, who frequently succeeded in breaking through the opposing lines of the foe, and this usually was the first step towards victory. Sometimes, if an overpowering stroke was intended, they made the first charge on the Scots at full gallop; but again, they often remained either behind the divisions of infantry, or near the flanks of the army, ready to enter whenever an opening was made in the opposite columns. Robert Bruce knew all this, and, with that penetrative wisdom for which he was so remarkable, began at once to introduce regular order among his men, enforcing them not to break the line of battle. It was in strict observance of this design that he was in a great measure indebted to his good fortune at Bannockburn.

General order was subsequently observed on commencing battle, both by the English and Scots, but in the heat of conflict it was occasionally neglected, for often 'groom fought like noble, squire like knight,' and every true man, from the king to the meanest soldier, performed his part therein to the best of his power. At Agincourt, Henry the Fifth was not only beaten down on his knees, but was 'repeatedly struck upon his helmet and armour,' and when 'his brother, the Duke of Gloucester, was felled senseless at his feet, the king immediately stood over him, repelled a long and furious attack to take him, and had the gratification to preserve his life.' (Turner vol. ii).

---

8. There was nothing peculiar to Scotland in tactics before the days of Robert Bruce.—*Innes.*

In England, among the various classes of combatants, the knights and men-at-arms, from the weight and force of their charge, as has been observed, were considered almost invincible. Through every nation in Europe, such warriors were renowned, for they usually came off victorious in battle; till in 1302, on the 11th July, near Courtray in Belgium, the brave Flemings, under John of Namur, encountered on foot the mailed chivalry of France, and won the victory, after which 4000 gilt spurs were found on the field. (*Serres*). Tidings of this change in the mode of warfare circulated all over the known world, so that Bruce drew conclusions from it, which were of essential service to himself through all his future career. In 1307, between two morasses east of Loudon Hill, his lines of serried spearmen repulsed the attack of a gallant body of English cavalry led by De Valence, Earl of Pembroke, and put them to flight.[9]

He had also the sagacity to perceive that Wallace was vanquished at the Battle of Falkirk, after his cavalry had shamefully fled, by the English knights and men-at-arms surrounding his bodies or schiltrums[10] of spearmen, and steadily destroying them after all chance of retreat for the unfortunate men was cut off. Weighing every circumstance, he thereby perceived his main chance of success lay in selecting a suitable piece of ground for battle whereon to place his army, so that they could not possibly be outflanked, but have sufficient room whereon to meet the enemy in deadly encounter. Valiant and powerful though Bruce was at any moment in the use of his weapons, he was at the same time wise, considerate, and cautious, never failing in judgment when an important case came before him, but, according to circumstances, ever deciding for the best.

---

9. The lowest morass, that to the south-east of the spot, is now drained and bearing crops. Kerr, in his *History of Scotland*, says, 'The spearmen were probably drawn up in a solid phalanx or deep battalion; and if arrayed in eight ranks, which long afterwards continued to be the order of such troops, six hundred men would present a front of seventy-five files, covering a space of about fifty yards, allowing two feet for each man.'—Vol. i.

10. *Schiltrum*, a mass of men, large or small, crowded together in a square or circular form.

CHAPTER 2

Mustering of Forces

After Edward the Second, in 1307, ascended the throne of England, instead of directing his attention to the wellbeing of his kingdom, he continued, as he had done in the lifetime of his father, to prefer the company of favourites to that of his nobility, and bestowed upon the former royal grants and rewards, whereby he incurred the displeasure and hostility of the latter. Differences accordingly arose between them, each carrying out their own measures; and during this period, when the English monarch partly relaxed his hold of the reins by which he held Scotland in subjection, Robert Bruce availed himself of the opportunity, and, by aid from his faithful adherents, strove to liberate that land from the thraldom which the first Edward had imposed upon it. He himself, from the time he was crowned at Scone in 1306, had undergone great privation both of body and mind; but a better prospect now opened up before him, and he took advantage of the occurrence, nobly turning it to the best account.

In 1310, the estates of Scotland,[1] actuated by Bruce, having met at Dundee, solemnly declared that Robert, Lord of Annandale, the competitor, ought by the laws of Scotland to have been preferred to Baliol in competition for the crown; and they recognised Robert Bruce, his grandson, now reigning, as their just and lawful king, engaging to defend his right and the independence of Scotland against all opponents of every rank or dignity; and declaring that whoever contravened the same should be guilty of treason, and held as traitors to the nation.[2]

A pastoral declaration was also issued by the representatives of the church, with the bishops and others, 'that the Scots nation, seeing the

---

1. *The Three Estates* of Parliament; the lords, including the prelates, the barons, and the burgesses.

2. Instrument in the General Register House, Edinburgh, alluded to by Kerr, vol. i.

kingdom betrayed and enslaved, had assumed Robert Bruce for their king, and that the clergy had willingly done homage to him in that character.' This, it would appear, was only a repetition of a manifesto issued previously by twelve bishops of Scotland, to which their names were all attached, and it ran nearly in the same words. By this means Bruce showed the greatest wisdom. He thereby disarmed the papal thunder of all its power, both in favouring England, and in endeavouring to crash himself and his fellow-patriots by excommunication. These measures were of immense consequence to him in the promotion of his design, and they had their full effect among a people who regarded the church with the utmost deference and respect.

About this time, or previously, according to Buchanan, Sir John de Menteith, who basely betrayed Wallace, still held possession of the castle of Dumbarton for the King of England. Robert Bruce was induced to enter into negotiation with him for its surrender, and Menteith demanded in return the earldom of Lennox. That honour was held by one of the king's steady supporters, who, when he came to know the proposed terms, generously insisted that his sovereign should complete the exchange. The agreement at length being solemnly ratified, Bruce went to receive possession of the place, and in passing the wood of Colquhoun near Dumbarton, Holland, a carpenter, sought an interview with him, and told him that a number of armed English were concealed in a cellar of the fortress, so that when the king sat down to dine, these were to come forth and either kill or make him prisoner. Accordingly, when Bruce had obtained the castle, and was looking through the several apartments therein, Menteith asked him to partake of an entertainment, which the king refused till the concealed cellar should be examined.

This Menteith attempted to evade by saying that a menial had the key, and would be there presently. Eventually, on breaking up the door, the treachery was revealed, and it was ascertained, that had the plan been successful, a ship was stationed in the firth ready to convey Bruce to England. The traitor was imprisoned, and had suffered death, which he well deserved, but having several beautiful daughters married to wavering but powerful noblemen in the neighbourhood, he was on their account spared. The result will be noticed hereafter. From the note quoted below[3] we vouch not for the truth of the statement,

---

3. Edward II., inclining to pacific measures, authorised, 2nd and 21st August 1309, Richard de Bury, Earl of Ulster, to treat with Bruce; who appointed Sir John de Menteith and Sir Nigel Campbell to conduct this treaty.'—*Foedera*, vol. iii., quoted by *Hailes*, ii.

but it deserves a place, connected as it is with the prowess and good fortune of the Scottish king.

From the trials to which the common people of Scotland were subjected, they became sensible of the inestimable value of freedom, and nobly supported their king in his attempts to rescue the country from bondage. In 1311, a small farmer named William Binnock, at or near Linlithgow, in company with a few armed friends, succeeded in wresting from the English the castle of that ancient town. Robert Bruce, in 1312, recovered from the enemy the castles of Dumfries, Dalswinton, Ayr, and Lanark, besides many other strongholds, the defenders of which, when his force was brought against them, found it desirable to submit to his power. A few months later he laid siege to Perth, and investing it for a time, he took the place near midnight, early in January 1313, himself crossing the ditch which surrounded it, while the water rose to his throat.

Very soon afterwards, James Douglas, lord of the valley of that name, by the assistance of his trusty followers, won from the enemy the strong fortress of Roxburgh on the eve of Lent, when the garrison therein were enjoying themselves in revelry. This occurred early in March, and on the week following, Thomas Randolph Earl of Moray, after closely investing the castle of Edinburgh, took it also during the night, by escalade, and as the design of Bruce was to demolish all places of defence which the English might possibly occupy, the walls of this and the other fortifications were speedily thrown down.

The castle of Bothwell still remained in possession of England, and this also might possibly have been taken, but another matter of greater importance was at hand. It would appear that Sir Edward Bruce, while his fellows in arms were accomplishing so much, had not been idle, for he captured the castles of Rutherglen and Dundee, and afterwards, in the spring of 1313, laid siege to the castle of Stirling. But the position of this fortress, for it was placed on the summit of a rock, and its natural defences on every side save one, rendered it almost impregnable. The brother of the king, however, continued to invest it till the middle of summer without any appearance of success, when Sir Philip Mowbray, the governor, a Scotsman in the service of England, arranged with him that if the fortress was not relieved till the nativity of Saint John the Baptist, 24th June of the following year, he would forthwith surrender it to the King of Scotland.

Sir Edward was remarkably brave, and a most resolute man, but he lacked the foresight and wisdom of his brother, who in the meantime had invaded Cumberland and conquered the Isle of Man. When the compact was reported to Bruce on his return home, he was very angry, because he at once perceived its impropriety. 'You have done wrong,' said he to his brother, 'and we shall all feel its evil effects, for by such an agreement you allow our powerful enemy a whole year to collect under arms the military force of all his provinces, while we of Scotland will have great difficulty to meet him in the field. Had you pressed Mowbray closely, and not assented to any such stipulation, Stirling Castle in all probability had been ours ere the present year expires.'

'I may have committed an error,' replied Sir Edward, 'but I did it for the best, and if all the warriors he of England can raise will come forward, we will undoubtedly give them battle.' 'Be it so, then,' observed the king, 'we must abide by what you have done. Honour is more dear than life to a true man, and we must do our utmost to confront the strength of England, come when it may.'

Sir Philip Mowbray, having been supplied with a safe-conduct for his journey to and from England, went to London and laid the whole affair before King Edward. Perceiving he was about to lose all ascendency in Scotland, that monarch, on due consideration, resolved to make a desperate effort to retain what had cost his father so much anxiety, and England an enormous amount of human life and treasure. He accordingly entered upon the necessary preparations for the accomplishment of his design, and that his force might be augmented to the greatest possible number, he pardoned all who were implicated in the death of Gaveston.[4] This was so acceptable to the English people, that the earls, barons, knights, and community granted the king, to enable him to carry on the war in Scotland, a twentieth, while the citizens and burgesses supplied him with a fifteenth of their goods. He likewise endeavoured to borrow money from the clergy to defray the cost of the expedition.

Directing his attention to the Continent, he sent for the bravest of his vassals from Gascony, and enlisted troops from Flanders and other foreign states which were in any way under his influence. In England he summoned all the great vassals of the crown, consisting of ninety-three barons, to bring with them the whole feudal force of the kingdom in arms, with horse and accompaniments, and meet him at Berwick, on Monday, the 10th June of the following year. (Summons

---

4. The document is dated at Westminster, 16th October 1313. The names occupy nearly four pages in the *Foedera*, vol. iii.

dated at Westminster, 23rd December 1313). Similar commands were also sent to the leaders of his English subjects in Ireland; and letters were directed to Eth O'Connor, Prince of Connaught, and twenty-five Irish chiefs, that they should muster their followers under Richard de Burgh, Earl of Ulster, and come over to assist him against Robert Bruce. (Dated at Westminster, 22nd March 1314). Two days afterwards he appointed Aymer de Valence, Earl of Pembroke, to be Governor of Scotland, and sent him thither to be ready on the royal arrival.

Commands were also issued to the mayors of the several seaport towns of England and Wales, that they should not only send forth the ships they had ready, but equip an additional fleet to assist in the war against the Scots. When the king, on his progress northward,[5] arrived at Newminster Abbey, near Morpeth, on the 27th May, he sent to the Sheriffs of York and seventeen other counties of England and Wales, orders to array 21,500 foot soldiers, who were to be at Werk on Tweedside, before the 10th June. (See note following).

Note:—It appears he had learned at this point of his journey, how and where Bruce intended to give him battle, as the following translation from the original order in Latin will show:—'The King to the Sheriff of Yorkshire wisheth health. As, for the expedition in our Scots war, we have chosen four thousand men from your county, whom we have ordered to attend us into Scotland on the day already mentioned, and as we now learn that the Scots, our enemies and rebels, are using their utmost efforts to collect a great multitude of infantry, in strong and marshy places, where access is difficult for cavalry; that, placing themselves between us and our castle of Stirling, they may thereby oppose the rescue of our said castle with all their power: which rescue must be made upon the next ensuing festival of the nativity of St. John the Baptist, according to the agreement entered into between the constable of our said castle and our said enemies; and which rescue, with the blessing of divine aid, we propose then to accomplish,' etc.—Foedera, vol. iii.

'The orders to the sheriffs and others having authority in the several counties of England and Wales, were extremely peremptory; and they were commanded to urge, hasten, and compel the

5. On Easter day, which fell on the 7th April, the king was at Ely; on the 20th April he was at Lincoln; on the 27th he was at Beverley; and at York from the 6th to the 12th of May. *Rot. Scot.*, vol. i..

several required quotas, under the highest penalties, to march in a state of sufficient preparation, and fitly armed, so as to join the royal army at Werk.'—Kerr, vol. i.

These bands of infantry, which the king so earnestly demanded, ought to have been with him some days previously, had his former mandates been observed. Besides all these forces, he had still many adherents in Scotland, who for their own interest performed his commands, and who were prepared to take their place in his ranks when he arrived in that country. Moreover, he invested John Duke of Argyle with the title of High Admiral of the western fleet of England; and, as that nobleman possessed many ships, he was appointed to cooperate with those of the king, that the whole movement might be perfect for the entire subjugation of the Scots. He had likewise to arrange that provision for the troops and forage for the cavalry should be provided in regular order throughout the course of his expedition. Numbers of masons, carpenters, smiths, and armourers, were also engaged to accompany the fighting men; while waggons, cars, and beasts of burden, were required to convey the pavilions, baggage, and other necessary articles of so large an army.

Robert Bruce and his adherents, heroic men, actuated by noble enthusiasm, did all in their power to increase the army of Scotland. Nearly all the people of the kingdom, save those of the eastern portion of Berwickshire, and on the coast northward beyond Dunbar, had submitted to the sway of Bruce, and, as has been observed, what told effectually toward his success, the clergy, judging truly of the important crisis, were wholly in his favour. Every intellectual Scotsman was aware how his country had been harassed and his fellow-men slaughtered by the English, while the murder of Wallace, the gallant, the patriotic, the devoted defender of all that was sacred in his own land, caused among his countrymen, who were 'trained to arms in stern misfortune's field,' an irrepressible feeling of wrath and resentment.[6] During a continued struggle of eight years, King Robert, by his prudence, prowess, and sagacity, caused them to hope that if they stood truly to him, and gave him all the support they could yield, better days were in prospect than any they had yet seen.

---

6. They were 'hardened with continual use of war, and, by reason that on the points of their swords and spears they carried along with them all their hopes of life, liberty, honour, and wealth, were unspeakably resolute and fierce. Besides, they had at their head a leader who alone was worth multitudes; nothing escaped the depth of his penetration and forecast.'—*Abercromby*, vol, i.

When a proclamation, therefore, went forth that the warriors of these districts of Scotland who were favourable to Bruce should come forward ready for battle, it was obeyed with wonderful celerity, and, considering the depressed state of the kingdom, with its lack of the very means of war, it seems astonishing how such numbers of active men could be drawn thence in defence of all that we in more favourable times hold venerable and dear.

Mention has been made of Sir John de Menteith being imprisoned on account of his treachery to Bruce. At this time, as the king had to 'contend for the safety of the State,' lest the noblemen who had married the daughters of the traitor should be incited to revenge, he liberated Menteith—'his sons-in-law being his sureties'—on condition that the wavering chieftain should take up his position in front of the first impending battle whenever it might take place.

King Edward would appear to have remained at Newminster Abbey till about the 7th day of June, and then proceeded to Berwick, where he lingered probably to receive the last levies of his great army from England and Ireland, On the 18th June he quitted Berwick with his forces, and held on his way to Edinburgh. When Robert Bruce heard he had crossed the Tweed with such a splendid array of martial men, he made arrangement that his whole power should instantly assemble at the Torwood, a few miles north-west of Falkirk. To this place of meeting Sir Edward Bruce came, and brought with him all the able men he could muster; so also did Walter the Steward and James Douglas, who exerted themselves most manfully in endeavouring to make Scotland free.

Nor was Randolph Earl of Moray behind his fellows in the noble enterprise, and the exertions of all to bring so many fighting men together were most gratifying to the gallant Bruce. He himself was accompanied by his devoted followers, and he found that the warriors who assembled round him numbered upwards of thirty thousand. Besides these, apart from the immediate attendants on the knights and cavalry, were the camp-followers of every description, who might amount to above fifteen thousand men. Here, on the openings among the trees, they had ample room for movement, for tradition says that Torwood once extended from the banks ox the Carron, in the parish of Dunipace, far into that of St. Ninian's, at Tor-brex, near Stirling. This range of greenwood, in the memory of many of these warriors, afforded shelter repeatedly to Wallace and his gallant followers, when hardly beset by the English under Edward the First.

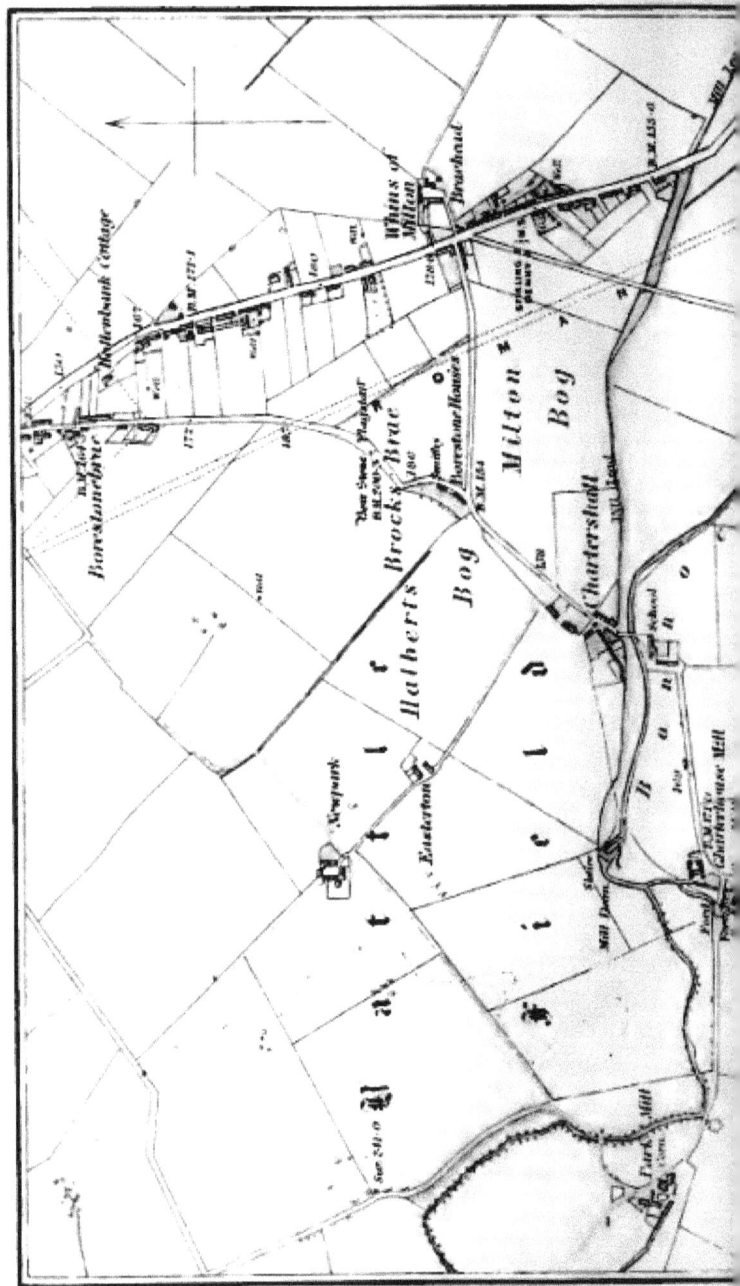

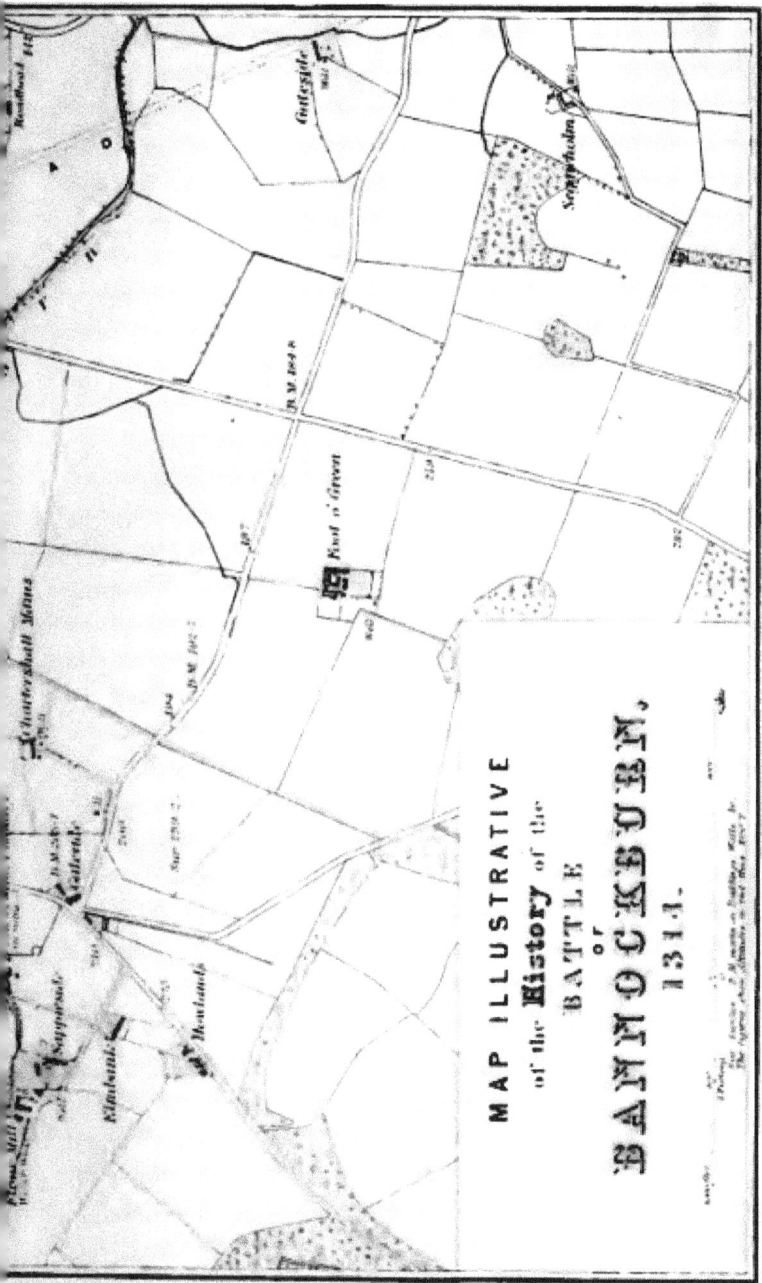

MAP ILLUSTRATIVE

of the **History** of the

BATTLE

of

BANNOCKBURN,

1314.

CHAPTER 3

Localities Connected With the Battle

When King Edward proceeded northward from Berwick with the whole martial strength of England, we learn from our most authentic chroniclers that no army of such magnitude had ever before crossed the Borders. Rejecting the account of one or two authors as undeserving of credit on that point, we may fairly estimate the number of the whole effective men to have been above one hundred thousand. Of these forty thousand were cavalry, including knights and men-at-arms, of whom more than a twelfth part had horses clothed in mail, who were intended to form the van in the field of battle. The archers are said to have numbered about fifty thousand, and the remainder consisted of billmen and spearmen, who in combat were to take their places between the divisions of the cavalry. Of the chief leaders expected by the king, four were absent, namely, the Earls of Lancaster, Warenne, Warwick, and Arundel, who alleged, by way of excuse, he had failed in performing to them certain promises, but they each sent their contingent of horsemen and infantry. In the order of march they were separated into ten divisions, each numbering about ten thousand armed men.

Much is left for our imagination to fill up when we contemplate the appearance of the great army of England wending its way over hill and dale, through forest and glade, by the banks of the streams and across the broad open wastes of the south of Scotland. A strain of lofty poetry is discernible in the verses of the venerable Archdeacon of Aberdeen, when he describes the pomp and magnificence of the splendid spectacle, under the rays of a bright summer sun. The chief warriors appeared in their most sumptuous array, with surcoats embroidered in various bright colours, exhibiting their respective bearings, and covering such plate armour as they then wore, while above them, fluttering in the breeze, was a forest extending for miles in every direction, of banners and flags, emblazoned in gold and other dazzling hues, and these again were everywhere intermingled still more densely with the long slender pennons and streamers of rich silk waving from the heads of the spears borne by the knights, who always held them aloft on the journey.[1] These were all marshalled in due order, according to the respective ranks of the nobles, and in strict conformity to the regulations of heraldry.

A troop of horsemen probably led the way first, then several squadrons of archers; then the king among his chief officers, heading the main divisions of cavalry, which covered many a broad acre, all mounted on strong horses; then followed large bodies of infantry intermingled with cavalry; and behind came the requirements of the camp, some borne on horseback, and a large portion on rude carriages drawn by oxen, mules, and horses. Of these the number seems to have been enormous, conveying as they did articles used in besieging castle or town, harness, victual, wine in cask and bottle, clothing and domestic utensils both for hall and chamber. The general impression seems to have been that the English would secure all Scotland to themselves, so that multitudes of the common people brought with them, as they best might, wife and child, pot and pan, pig and poultry.

Among the crowd of travellers was one individual, Robert Baston by name, a Carmelite friar of Scarborough, who being accounted a good Latin versifier, came by order of the king to celebrate in imperishable lines the conquest of Scotland. Whether on his way he stretched himself to rest at night beside the joiner and smith, like the two minstrels of Northumberland's Earl in the sixteenth century, or he slept among better company, we have no means of knowing. Through the whole course of the progress of King Edward on this expedition, he seems to have been so elevated by the enormous numbers of his army, that he firmly believed the Scots were unable to offer any resistance to his arms. The general conversation in almost every class was, how Scotland was to be disposed of, and it was arranged they would take Robert Bruce with his brother Edward, and convey them to London, to be dealt with as they deserved.[2]

1. But King Edward and his people seemed rather to go towards a *wedding*, or a *triumph*, than to a battle, adorning themselves with all sorts of riches, gold, silver, and the like toyes, in a kind of wanton manner, correspondent to the humour of the prince whom they followed.—*Speed.*

2. The whole strength of England produced such a confidence in every breast that the universal topic of conversation with this vast assemblage was not so much about carrying on the war, as about dividing the spoil.—*Buchanan,* vol. i.

After this manner the King of England and his council spoke only of appropriating the plunder, so that Scotland might be divided among those of the army and others who were best deserving of such reward. In this case, according to the adage, they 'reckoned without the host,' for as our favourite author quaintly observes,—

Or thai cum all to thair entent,
Howis iu haile claith sall be rent.

There can be no doubt that, with the view of resisting the power of England, Robert Bruce had most carefully examined the whole vicinity of the way to Stirling, and, acquiring wisdom from the former battles in which he had been engaged, deemed it of the utmost importance to select a place most suitable to his purpose. Knowing the main object of King Edward was to press forward and relieve the castle there, he had to choose it in the likeliest line through which the English would attempt to pass, and prevent them reaching that fortress by any other route. Moreover, he had the privilege of causing the enemy to fight him on ground most advantageous to himself, and accordingly he fixed on the gentle slope of Bannockmoor, so called by the common people at that time, for his battlefield, which was within the New Park, about two miles southward from Stirling. Here, however, it may be necessary to give the reader some account of the approach from Edinburgh to the latter place, and more particularly of the plot of land whereon the great conflict was decided.

We doubt not but considerable light might be thrown on the boundaries of New Park, could access be obtained to the charter-chests of the proprietors of the ground in that neighbourhood, or into the ancient records of the borough of Stirling. From the *Chamberlain's Accounts* we learn that:

In 1263 the Sheriff of Stirling was employed in repairing the ancient park, and in constructing a new park there for Alexander III., and was allowed in his column of expenditure an outlay on that head of £80. Twenty years later there was an allowance for two park-keepers and one hunter of wolves at Stirling, and for the expenses of four hundred perches, (twenty-two hundred yards), of palisade round the new park; and for mowing and carrying hay and litter for the use of the fallow deer in winter.

Again, Barbour relates that Sir Robert Clifford, when on his way to Stirling with his gallant troop of horse, *eschewit* or avoided the New Park, wending his way onward beneath it, and also beneath the kirk, meaning that of St. Ninian's. Also the same author observes that when King Edward with his nobles betook themselves to flight on leaving Stirling, they *enweround*, or went round the park in all haste towards Linlithgow. It would appear to have comprised a large tract of land, consisting of hill, dale, lake, and stream. Scotland's kings had kept it for the preservation of beasts of the chase, so that when they resided at Stirling they might enjoy the sports of the field cither with falcon or hound. Wild animals found shelter in the higher uplands among the trees growing there, while the burn, the swamps, the wells, and their courses below, must have been the resort of water-fowl of every description.

In all likelihood it included the mountain range round by Gillies' Hill, the land chiefly covered with wood on each side of the Bannock for above a couple of miles, the Halbert and Milton Bogs, and in its eastern circuit, sweeping round the lower grounds, by the mills of Milton[3] towards the present town of Bannockburn, and near to the village of St. Ninian's. Probably the roads, if that by the Bore-stone was then formed, might be diverted round by its eastern extremity. We may likewise suppose that in 1314 the enclosures would be almost wholly broken down in the course of oppression which Scotland sustained from the first Edward, but within its limits, and especially on Bannockmoor, where the battle was to be fought, were portions of woodland, not a few, which Bruce considered would mar the charges of the English horse; and even at the present day the farm-steading erected on the lower portion of the field, where Walter the Steward and Sir James Douglas repelled the squadrons of the enemy, still bears the name of New Park.

The castle of Stirling was erected on the top of a lofty massive trap-rock, that rises abruptly from the level ground all round it, save on the south-east side, while on the north-east are some hilly eminences of lower elevation, but from these the castle is separated by the deep hollow of Ballangeich. On the north-west and north the sides of the rock are highest, presenting a series of lofty blocks of naked stone, rising almost perpendicularly above each other. Like the fortress at Edinburgh,

---

3. Bannocksborne, so named of oten-cakes called bannocks, which were used to bee made commonlie at the mils standing on the banks of the said water.—*Hollinshed*. Modern etymologists will say the word is derived from a different source than that ascribed to it by the old chronicler.

the soil on its south-eastern side descends gradually from the summit down nearly to the level of the surrounding plain.

Again, at a short distance from the bottom of this slope, a gentle rise takes place nearly southward, and, with some undulations, it continues about half-a-mile beyond St. Ninians, till the top of the height is reached near to the Bore-stone at Caldam Hill. Still farther east, towards the Whins of Milton, the rise continues, and behind this whole elevation, stretching from north-west to south-east, were Halbert's Bog and Milton Bog, the bottoms of which are now dry; but at an early period both formed, in all likelihood, one lake, which neither man nor horse could pass over.[4] Southward again from these sheets of water, Bannockburn, descending from the hills westward, flows down in an easterly direction to Milton, and on passing the mills there, bends northward, entering a deep ravine, which continues downward past the village bearing the name of the stream, till it winds through the level carse onward to the Forth.

The most direct route, therefore, from Falkirk to Stirling, by the only road apart from the broad carse, was over the piece of land between the lower end of Milton Bog and the head of the defile close to the village of Milton. The Roman road or street lay through this ground, which was only about five hundred yards in width, hence it was somewhat narrow for the passage of a large army, besides, the lead to the mills ran directly athwart it, and the Bannock had to be crossed, which ran amid moist boggy soil, the banks of which were high and broken.

The other, and indeed the only remaining approach for an army such as that of England, was higher up the stream, from the vicinity of Chartres Hall up to Park Mill, averaging a width of nearly half-a-mile, where the banks sloped to the burn, and where the latter could be easily passed over. Below the former place, the Bannock ran low among soil and slake, while another broad morass or lake also stretched from its south-western margin to the rise of the ground immediately below Foot o' Green.

Above Park Mill, again, the left bank of the burn, on looking downward, was almost impassable, not so much by rising abruptly from the stream to a considerable height, but from being covered northward, from the channel thereof to the high land overhanging it, with dense underwood and trees. Moreover, about a quarter of a mile above Park Mill, and in a northern direction, the Bannock descends

4. See Appendix. Note A.

from the west, forming nearly a right angle, for it rashes into and again flows down southward from the base of a lofty bank. It was from the rounded summit of this bank, down eastward in a gentle slope to the head of Halbert's Bog, measuring about eight hundred yards, where Bruce determined he should behold his warriors first strike for liberty.[5]

Low down beneath him, on his right hand, hidden, yet giving forth notes of sweet melody among wood and bramble, the Bannock flowed to the south, while at a distance of above half-a-mile, away on his left, stretched the line of Halbert's and Milton bogs, gleaming with water. Before him the land descended, for nearly six hundred yards, gradually to the stream, which here wended again in an easterly direction, and on this plot of ground, nearly half-a-mile square, himself and his patriotic army had ultimately the good fortune to establish by arms the freedom and independence of Scotland.

Occupying this position, and knowing the sanguine anticipations of the King of England, Robert Bruce foresaw that if the enemy made no attempt to approach Stirling by the carse, which was unlikely, from the moistness of the soil, for portions of it might be under water, and thick underwood probably grew on and around it, but advanced by the main road, he would here await and take the fortune that God would send.

One point he perceived must be dealt with, and that was to block up or render impassable the open space or thoroughfare at Milton, and if the road by the Bore-stone was then formed, to operate upon it in the same manner. Were either one or both open, a few troops of English horse might cross over, and not only throw succour into the castle of Stirling, but, while the Scottish forces were contending in battle, surround or attack them in flank or rear.

Therefore, Bruce, believing himself, in the place he had selected, to be secure on the right, and thus defending his position on the left, the English must of necessity be compelled to meet his army face to face.[6] In this field he had ample room to bring into action the whole of his forces, and it was impossible his wings could be outflanked or surrounded by the enemy. The lines of his divisions might have been extended on a wider space, but if in any way they were confined, he had the sagacity to foresee that the English would be still more so, for

---

5. Bruce posted himself where he had a hill on his right flank, and a morass on his left.—*Hume*, vol, iii.

6. The time and place were fixed by an obdurate necessity.—*Burton*, vol ii.

not another opponent could enter into conflict than the front ranks who met his own spearmen.[7] Hereby the huge multitude of invaders who were behind would of course be crowded together in unwieldy masses, cumbering rather than taking part in the efficient movement of the whole.

---

7. Battles are decided not by troops upon the muster rolls, nor even by those present, but by those alone who are simultaneously engaged. Numerical superiority of troops not engaged, so far from being useful, only increases the disorder.'—*Suppt. Encyclop. Britannica*, 1824, vol. vi. article on 'War' by Major C. H. Smith.

CHAPTER 4

Advance of the Scots to New Park

On Friday the 21st June,[1] King Robert still lingering in the Torwood, went through and most carefully examined his whole army, speaking to those near him words of great kindness, in the full assurance that when the approaching struggle came their efforts would be crowned with success. To the chief officers who formed his privy council he communicated his arrangement for battle. He first pointed out the great importance of preventing any detachment of the enemy moving forward to the aid of Stirling Castle.

Next he observed that when the thoroughfare at Milton was closed, the English, on their approach, must needs advance about half-a-mile farther up on the south-west side of the Bannock, till they crossed it, where they would be encountered at great advantage. The Scottish force they knew amounted to above thirty thousand fighting men, and if these were separated into four divisions, should their enemies attempt to pass over or near the morass, which, if it were possible, could only be done either singly or by a limited number at once, they would be met and readily overcome. Moreover, he deemed it exceedingly desirable that they should go lightly armed on foot to battle, for the English, being more powerful, rode better horses, and did the Scots attempt to encounter them with cavalry, the result might be attended, with great peril. Therefore, if they fought on foot, they could take advantage of the ground, for several clumps of trees were on Bannockmoor, which, with the open swamps and watercourses below,[2] would cumber and put their assailants to great perplexity.

---

1. In 1314 Midsummer day fell on Monday the 24th of June, being that of the nativity of St. John the Baptist.

2. In all probability the margins of the lake or lakes of Halbert and Milton Bogs, together with the grounds through which Bannockburn flowed, (cont. next page),

To these suggestions the leaders readily agreed, while Bruce knew well the importance of availing himself of their counsel on every case of emergency. Of the four companies into which it was proposed the army should be portioned, the van or central division[3] in the line of battle, they committed to the leadership of Randolph Earl Moray, whose troops were drawn probably from the lands bordering on the Moray Firth, and from the valleys of Nairn, Findhorn, and the rapid Spey. Beneath his banner several of the lords and chief men of the kingdom were stationed. The right wing was entrusted to the guidance of Sir Edward Bruce, whose bravery in every instance merited the highest praise, for our venerable chronicler graphically observes that whatever the result of the conflict might be, his opponents would have ample cause of lamentation. His forces, brave almost as himself, were likely brought from those parts of Scotland which lay beyond the influence of his martial brethren in arms.

On young Walter the Steward, and James Douglas, devolved the command of the left wing, the former having been instructed in warfare by the latter—a proven warrior—and this body consisted chiefly of tried Border warriors, accustomed from childhood to the use of battle-axe and spear, together with about one-third part of mountaineers from the north of Scotland. The fourth and last section of the army, Robert Bruce designed to take under his own charge, and these were his tried men of Carrick, of Argyle, Angus Lord of Kintyre and the isles, with a large number from the plain land.[4] Those, therefore, near to Milton, were soft and spongy. From the drainage and improvement of land which has taken place within the last century, we of the present day can scarcely form an idea of the number of 'joggle-beds,' 'well-eyes,' and quagmires, which existed all over the laud in former times. An old man told the author many years ago, that in early life he lived on a small farm in an upland district, and almost every other day, during summer, it was necessary to have a couple of horses and ropes at hand to drag out some young cow or horse, which, in seeking the fresh grass, had sunk in one of these places, and was of itself unable to get out.

3. Barbour and the chroniclers, who have written on the great struggle at Bannockburn, seemed to have considered the central division usually formed the van of an army in battle. It was intended so in this field, but in several other battles, including those of Neville's Cross and Agincourt on the side of England, the right wing, as has been already stated, had the honour of forming the van.

4. Angus M'Donald, Lord of the Isles and Kintyre, in 1306 received Bruce into his castle of Dunaverty, and protected him for nine months in his country of Rachlin, Isla, and Uist. In consequence of this never-to-be-forgotten fidelity, the King bestowed upon him as a reward the honour of taking the right hand in the Battle of Bannockburn. His clan enjoyed this privilege from that time, with exception of the Battle of Harlaw in 1411, when it was given to the, (continued next page),

with the king were to form the rearward, and from the elevated ground which they afterwards occupied, they must have been stationed behind Sir Edward Bruce and Randolph, ready to give help where it was required. In addition to the said divisions of troops, a large number of archers were also to be placed ready for battle, and above five hundred cavalry were to be at hand, that their force might be applied where it was most effective. These horsemen the king had especially appointed to perform a certain exploit, which will be related hereafter.

Robert Bruce, availing himself of the wisdom and experience of the chief men around him, made every arrangement for battle. Next day being Saturday, the 22nd June, on learning by his scouts that the English had come to Edinburgh and passed the night there, he gave orders that the whole army should move on towards Bannockmoor, which they did by the Roman road that led through the Torwood onward to the north, and lay a little to the west of Stirling. This causeway descended in a straight line from the west side of the farm-steadings of Snabhead and Pirnhall, crossed the Bannock, passed within a short distance east of the Bore-stone, and continued through the hollow on a part of the road between Coxet Hill and St. Ninians. But, as has been stated, a part of it from near Milton to the latter place was probably comprised within the New Park, and though the fences thereof might be destroyed, the locality would still retain the same name.

Accordingly, when the army came to Milton, the king caused a number of active men, accustomed to the spade in agriculture, to dig a series of deep pits, close together like a honeycomb, across the neck of laud from the lower end of Milton Bog to the lofty banks of the burn below that village.[5] Both the ancient Roman way, and probably a more recent road, which may have been made to the east of the New Park when it was enclosed, were thus cut through, that all pas-

Laird M 'Clean, and that of Culloden, but they took their position on the right both at Gladsmuir and Falkirk.—Lockhart Papers, vol. ii. This gallant chieftain, with his followers, must either have remained with the king, and fought in his presence during the battle, or taken his place on the right side of the warriors led by Sir Edward Bruce.

5. Barbour's words 'And in a plane field, be the way' can have only two meanings. One may be that the pits were dug in a plain field, close by the way whereon Bruce and his army went to the New Park. The other may signify that the plain field was near the Roman *way*, or old road, which was undoubtedly observable through the whole district at that early date. If any critic can elicit another meaning from the expression, I shall be glad to know it. Besides, the holes were made for the express purpose of preventing the enemy going through the park to the castle.

sage thereon, or near them, might be prevented. When those pitfalls were excavated, Bruce ordered them to be covered first with branches of trees, and above these green turf to be laid, and the earth so scattered about as not to show where the hollows really were.[6] If the road at Brock's Brae was then formed, we may presume it was broken up, and the pits concealed in the same manner. Had these cavities been left open, the reader will perceive how easily the English might have caused them to be filled up, so that no obstacle then could have prevented them passing over. The Scots were occupied in digging them all night, and had them completed next morning.

About this time we may conclude the Scottish Army occupied the height from the Whins of Milton to Caldam Hill, with the hollow west of it, up to Coxet Hill, and if the staff of the royal standard of Scotland was ever planted in the Bore-stone, the broad folds of that banner must have waved from it during that Saturday afternoon.[7] A few troops might be placed on the spot selected for battle, which was soon to be trodden down and flowing with human blood, but Bruce, we suspect, had the sense to leave that as it were open, till he saw the English advance, and if they took possession of the opposite ground near Foot o' Green and its vicinity, all would appear favourable.

Still he was uncertain by what way or in what order they would approach, so that he could only hold his own army in readiness to meet them, and guard the passage to the fortress of Stirling. He took no rest during the night, but wandered about from one portion of his army to another, revolving in his mind the circumstances in which he was placed, and the bearing they might have on the future of Scotland, yet providing for all that might occur, and trusting to a higher power than that of man, so that when the shock of battle came these heroic men around him might be enabled eventually to achieve the freedom of their native land.

---

6. It is improbable that Bruce, by the aid even of his chaplain, ever had *Herodotus* translated to him; but that author relates an incident almost similar to what was practised by the Scottish king. 'There is,' says he, 'a pass near the city of Hyampolis, where the Phocians, having dug a broad trench, filled up the void with empty wine-jars, after which they covered the place with mould, so that the ground all looked alike, and then awaited the coming of the Thessalians. These, thinking to destroy the Phocians at one sweep, rushed rapidly forward, and became entangled in the wine-jars, which broke the legs of their horses.'—*Herodotus*, vol. iv.
7. See Appendix. Note B.

CHAPTER 5

Commencement of Hostilities

Next morning, on Sunday, the 23rd of June, not long after the sun arose, the whole army of Scotland were collected, and they heard mass, which was celebrated in suitable order by the clergy who were present. Many confessed their sins most devoutly, and made solemn preparation either to offer up their lives in the impending struggle, or free their land from a foreign yoke. To the Most High earnest prayers were put up for assistance, and, as the result proved, these orisons happily were not offered in vain.

The day, be it remembered, preceded that of St. John the Baptist, and as the stern reality of battle was at hand they all fasted, resigning themselves to the keeping of their Maker, and allaying hunger on a little bread and water.

We who have come after, and enjoy, to the fullest extent, all the blessings of liberty, ought ever to be most thankful to God, and not less grateful to the memory of our glorious ancestors, who, in the face of privation and death, nobly won us that inheritance, which, under the auspices of heaven, we and our successors shall always be enabled resolutely to maintain.

When the solemnity performed by the priests was over, the king went and examined the pits which were then completed, and saw them on each side of the way done to his approval. He was convinced that if any troop of horsemen attempted to force a passage in this direction, they would find the undertaking more difficult than they at first contemplated.

But the time drawing near when the English would approach, King Robert, by way of showing his army the exact order of battle, and the ground they were to occupy, gave orders they should arm themselves speedily, and he led them to the locality he had selected, on which their valour was shortly to be put to the proof. Wending round the northern verge of Halbert's Bog, and ascending to the west in the direction of the northern angle of Bannockburn, above Park Mill and towards Graystale, each division in lines came to occupy the position on which they were to meet the enemy; and this was done that no confusion might ensue when the eventful hour of conflict arrived.

And now King Robert, with the design of rendering his cause most popular, ordered proclamation to be made that of all the fighting men assembled there, whoever feared his heart would fail him in the ensuing struggle, and who had not resolved either to win all or die with honour, was at liberty to quit the ranks instantly and depart home. He wished only, he observed, to have true and gallant heroes with him, who would do their utmost for the welfare of Scotland, and remain with him throughout the crisis, to take the fortune that God would vouchsafe to the noble and the brave. On this being known, a loud shout of exultation arose from the whole army, and the general cry was that none should fail, but remain firm to the last, in order to achieve the liberty of their country.

Hereupon the king enjoyed great satisfaction, being convinced he could place the utmost dependence on the bravery and patriotism of his men. Apart from the regular army above mentioned, there were nearly twenty thousand of men, women, and grown-up lads, who had charge of victual, harness, and other necessary articles, and who followed the camp on every occasion. These, with the stores for general use, were sent away to the west, up what is now called Gillie's Hill, to a small valley leading northward to the higher ground there, in order to be concealed from the view of the English, and with these, we are inclined to suppose, Bruce had also an especial purpose to perform.

When the king had thus placed his army in due order of battle, he learned that on the previous night, that of Saturday, the English had advanced to Falkirk, and were coming straight onward to Stirling. Accordingly, we suspect, the several battalions withdrew from line and shifted position, but were ready to form again whenever it was necessary.

They chiefly fell back in the direction of St. Ninians, and Bruce, in order to prevent the English from throwing by stratagem any succour into Stirling Castle, notwithstanding the precaution already taken of digging the pits, appointed Randolph, with a sufficient force, to keep the way near to the kirk, at the former place. He observed that himself and his brother, with the Steward, would prevent them approaching in any other direction.[1]

It was an anxious time for Bruce, for he despatched James Douglas and Sir Robert Keith Marischal, to observe the appearance of the English, so that, taking a few horse with them, they advanced in the direction of the Torwood, and very soon came in view of the enemy. To these warriors it was a splendid and magnificent sight. In every direction to the south-east, so far as the openings amid trees extended, shields, helmets, and lances innumerable, were everywhere sparkling in the rays of the sun—banners, standards, and the pennons attached to whole forests of spears, waved in the breeze. The gorgeous and rich dresses in almost every bright colour, worn by countless knights, were dazzling to behold, while squadrons beyond counting, on horse and foot, far as the eye could discern, might suffice to impress with awe the most mighty power in Christendom.

Douglas and Keith thereupon rode back to the king, and on telling him of the beauty, the splendour, and the gorgeous equipment of the English in untold numbers, he cautioned them not to divulge what they had witnessed, but to intimate that the foe, though numerous, approached in the utmost disorder. Bruce well knew it was necessary to put the best construction on the tidings, giving the army, by his looks and manner, perfect assurance that all would be well; and they also, apart from the justice of their cause, having implicit confidence in his ability as a leader, concluded that whatever opposition they might encounter, the struggle would eventually terminate in their favour. At this time we may suppose, that while waiting the advance of the English, and ready to do battle with them, the Scottish forces were ranged not only on the battlefield, but on the height near the Bore-stone, the cavalry were at hand, and the king himself being on horseback, in company with one or two of his leaders, that he might observe every hostile movement, whether from the south or east, occupied the summit of Coxet Hill.

Soon afterwards the waving banners of the English were descried on the heights near Plean, and behind Snabhead, and as they advanced and saw the Scots occupying the New Park, the chief leaders consulted together, and determined, if possible, to relieve the castle of Stirling. To accomplish this enterprise, they selected a troop of eight

---

1. We have here additional proof that Robert Bruce expected the English, on their way to Stirling, would pass either upon or near the Roman road. His care to have the pits dug at Milton points to the same conclusion. The said way, as has been stated, held its course a little to the west of the kirk and village of St. Ninians.

hundred horsemen, youthful and brave, who ardently aspired to distinguish themselves, and these, in charge of three barons accustomed to arms, among whom was Henry Beaumont, were arrayed under command of Sir Robert Clifford, a tried warrior. They saw many battalions of the Scots arrayed both on the ground selected for battle, and on the height west of the Whins of Milton, but suspecting that Bruce was there, the troop of horse under Clifford, hid from view by trees which grew on the low ground between them and Milton, threaded their way either near to the spot whereon the present bridge stands, or by the little valley in front of Craigford, and diving into the defile, swept past the place on which the house of Hill Park stands, and, favoured by the rising ground on the left, held on unobserved beneath the New Park direct for Stirling.

Advancing, however, below the church of St. Ninians, Clifford's horse came more into view, and the eagle-eye of Bruce detecting them, he gave orders for the Scottish cavalry to advance, and riding forward to Randolph, who was on the lower ground, told him he had permitted the enemy to pass, observing in the symbolic language of chivalry that 'a rose had fallen from his chaplet.'[2]

By this time Clifford's troop had advanced so far as to be between Randolph and Stirling, and as it was impossible for infantry to overtake them, the latter leader headed the Scottish horse, and led them instantly in pursuit. Clifford, perceiving the Scots behind him, caused his horsemen to wheel round and give them battle. (See note following).

Note:—Among the authorities who say that Randolph took cavalry with him are these:—*Buchanan*, vol. i.; *Hollinshed*; *Godscroft*. Also *Nisbet*, in his account of the family of Keith, vol. ii., appendix,, says—'At the Battle of Bannockburn he (Sir Robert Keith) commanded 500 horse, and gave the first onset, and defeat a party of English horse sent to reinforce Philip Mowbray, governor of Stirling, which made way for that glorious victory King Robert obtained in the above mentioned place.' Others, even down to the present day, including Tytler, Scott (*Hist, of*

---

2. A chaplet is a string of beads used by Roman Catholics in reciting the Lord's prayer, etc., and Lord Hailes imagines that *rose* implies the large bead therein for distinguishing a *Pater Noster* from an *Ave Maria.*—*Annals*, vol, ii. The phrase, we suspect, is less involved. Randolph, by his bravery, had gained distinction, and the king likened this to a chaplet of flowers for the hero's brow, among which roses were intertwined—hence, probably, the allusion.

Scotland), and Taylor, tell us they were spearmen or infantry. Barbour, in relating the circumstance, says the English were 'on fair coursers,' and that Randolph went against them with 'five hundred,' whereby he might mean horse without expressly saying so. Many historians follow their predecessors without thinking on the subject they are handling, and the following points deserve investigation.

Is it likely that a body of men on foot could overtake a troop of cavalry who had passed by to some distance ere they were pursued? What probability is there that the five hundred horsemen with Bruce remained idle when a circumstance of this kind occurred, for which they were specially adapted? Besides the perspiration, the breath, and the dust which, according to Barbour, arose in the midst of men and horse during the conflict, was it possible, as we learn afterwards, that footmen could outstrip and cut down those mounted English who, when defeated, were last in the flight? The whole achievement, from whatever point it may be seen, must, of course, come within the limits of probability.

We are unable to say whether Randolph ordered his men to dismount and fight on foot, placing their horses behind them, or to meet the enemy in the saddle, but he caused them to form a circle and draw up side by side, with their spears protruding outward, and thus withstand the assault of the foe.[3] The shock was serious; Sir William Daynecourt, being first in the onset, was instantly slain. The others came on more leisurely, and attempted time after time to break through the barrier of Scottish lances, but always with a loss to themselves. It seemed marvellous how the defensive band maintained its position, surrounded by such heavy-armed assailants; still they did so, and acquitted themselves most bravely. No impression could be made upon them, while the horses of the English, as they neared the fatal ring, being pierced probably by the longer weapons of the Scots,

---

3. The spot where this memorable conflict took place is still called 'Randolph's Field,' and is situated halfway between St. Ninians and Stirling, on the west side of the turnpike road. This proves the English had advanced to a considerable distance ere they were overtaken by the Scots. Fortunately, the place is marked by two large upright stones, which had been set up as memorials of Randolph's victory over Clifford's troop. We have, therefore, cause of regret that the site of the later and still more glorious battlefield was not indicated to future ages by some enduring landmarks of the same kind.

reared and threw their riders, who were trampled under foot and destroyed.

Some again of the Scots, when opportunity occurred, broke forward from their fellows, and dealing deadly blows both on horse and man, fell backward again to complete the defensive line of opposing steel. When the English perceived they could not break through the front of these northern warriors, they threw among them, with the utmost fury, maces, swords, and daggers, till the very weapons were piled above each other. As the struggle continued, the day being warm, the perspiration poured out over men and horses, and the dust arose above them like clouds at every fresh attempt to dash through the impenetrable circle. Yet not a man gave way, and every onset only occasioned additional loss to the English. The desperate struggle was intently observed by Bruce, one or two of whose chief leaders were near him, and at last, seeing no chance for Randolph in the midst of such an array, Douglas, though these heroes at that instant were not on terms of intimate friendship, besought the king that he might take a number of men and render his fellow-officer assistance. 'You shall not move,' said Bruce, 'for I will not alter my order of battle; let Randolph acquit himself as he best may.'

'I cannot stand here and see him overcome,' observed Douglas, 'so with your leave I must aid him whatever befall.'

'Go then,' said the king, 'but return speedily, for even now I require all the assistance I can command.'

Douglas thereupon departed, taking with him a number of infantry, but observing, as he approached the conflict, that the English were in confusion, and on the point of defeat, for many saddles were empty, he forbore to advance farther, saying, 'The Earl of Moray is about to overcome the enemy, and we must not presume to share in his well-earned glory. Let us return to the king, for he requires our help!' Then without delay he withdrew the men towards the main army.

CHAPTER 6

Sir Henry de Bohun Killed

Douglas had spoken the truth, for Robert Bruce, on observing that the English army was advancing in a north-western direction, gave orders that his own troops should move forward and occupy the ground he had specially selected for them. King Edward, when he came near to Snabhead, must have tarried for a time among his chief men, and observed not only the castle of Stirling, which stood full in view on its summit of rock, but marked the several divisions of the Scots, for he could scarcely believe, on considering his own enormous strength, that they would have the assurance to oppose him in actual conflict. Besides, only a portion of his forces must have come up, for they would occupy miles of road, and his carriages and waggons were still moving westward nearly all the way from Falkirk.

Nor is it improbable that another squadron of his cavalry, by way of trying the lines of approach, ventured to force a passage by Milton, and found it ineffectual. Forward, however, moved the army, till at length King Edward had himself probably come to the sloping ground near to Foot o' Green, when he ordered a halt to be made, in order that he might take counsel with his leaders whether they would rest that night to recruit the strength of the troops, or go forward and instantly commence the battle.

The Earls of Gloucester[1] and Hereford, who led the van, not being aware of the command to halt, led on their squadrons of horse till they crossed the Bannock and ascended the acclivity in the direction of the Scottish lines. Robert Bruce, in the absence of Randolph, had marshalled his battalions, as has been stated, on the space they were

---

1. Gloucester rode a beautiful horse, a present from the king, who received it as a gift from Richard Kellow, Bishop of Durham.

to occupy, and being mounted on a small but active horse, he rode along the front of his divisions fully armed, wearing a light crown of gold on his basinet, and having a battle-axe in his hand. Not expecting any immediate assault, he spoke words of comfort to his soldiers; and, to those near him, gave every assurance of victory. By this time it is likely the foremost of the English horse had approached to within a short distance from Bruce, when a valiant knight, Sir Henry Bohun, who was cousin to the Earl of Hereford, observing King Robert aloof from his troops, and being ambitious of accomplishing a notable feat of arms, spurred his war-horse toward him, supposing he might either kill him or take him prisoner.

When the heroic king, who had come off unscathed from many encounters of this kind, saw him make the attempt, the spirit of the old Adam so roused his heart and braced his nerves that he met him in the shock, but turning his horse slightly to the left, he parried the point of De Bohun's lance, and swinging his axe round, with a tremendous blow, crashed the helmet and brain of his opponent, laying him dead among his charger's feet.

In the haste and heat of the moment, though the edge of the steel effectually accomplished the king's purpose, the stroke had been dealt somewhat obliquely, for the shaft of the weapon was broken in his grasp. This passage of arms was witnessed by both armies, and accordingly the front ranks of the Scots took heart, and, raising a great shout, advanced with their spears before them, but the English withdrew, being dismayed on observing their daring adventurer so speedily overcome, though a few were overtaken and killed. On recalling the Scottish pursuers, the chief men around the king blamed him for putting his life in jeopardy when the battle had yet to be struck; but he, fully aware of the importance of the charge, turned it aside by expressing his sorrow that he had shivered the handle of his good battle-axe.

By this time the Earl of Moray had succeeded in vanquishing Lord Clifford's cavalry, many saddles were empty, and around lay a heap of men and horses wounded and dying. The English had drawn back by degrees, and on taking the direct way to their own countrymen, several of the lingerers last in the flight were pursued, and either taken or slain.[2] When the Scots found they were victorious, they leisurely raised their basinets, and wiping the perspiration from their faces, as-

---

2. Among the prisoners was Sir Thomas Gray of Heton, to whose son we are indebted for the translation from French rhyme into French prose of the valuable history entitled *Scalacronica.*—*Raine.*

certained their loss was very slight, though we can scarcely be induced to believe it amounted only to one man. On Randolph rejoining the army, Robert Bruce, learning of his success in performing such a gallant achievement, gave him and the cavalry a most hearty welcome, while the other warriors crowded around, anxious to behold such noble heroes, and awarding them the honour and glory which they so justly deserved.

On the English being thrown back in both these instances, Bruce collected his chief men around him, and again admonished them to take heart—to praise and love the Almighty, for such a prosperous beginning indicated a favourable termination. The success, he observed, already won would operate to the discomfort and dismay of their adversaries, more especially as the troop under Clifford consisted of the most powerful and courageous men in the English Army. Good fortune, no doubt, from the sacred cause for which Scotland fought, would attend her gallant sons; and here again he appealed to his adherents, as he did not say this that his own desire for battle might be followed, but he was ready in every respect to do as those around him should recommend for the welfare of themselves and their country, and therefore he wished them to give free expression to their thoughts.

On the instant a shout arose from the listeners near, who declared that if no assault on the part of England took place that evening, they wished the good king to place them in order of battle on the morning of the following day, and that neither trial nor dread of death should move them in any way till they had given freedom to their own land. Bruce was delighted on hearing this expression of patriotic daring, and rejoicing in their valour and hardihood, he observed that since it was their desire, they should array themselves for fight next morning, and, on hearing mass, each man would take his place under the displayed banner of his respective leader.

CHAPTER 7

Preparation for Battle

By way of admonishing his chief men and those near him how the battle should be conducted, and of acquainting them with his own opinion of the crisis at hand, the king continued to say that of one thing especially he would remind them, which was, not to break the array, for no man must go beyond the line of his own comrades, else disaster would ensue.[1] Also, as they respected him, when they came front to front with the foe, each man with his whole heart and might would, he trusted, do the very utmost in his power to overthrow the strength of the English. They would come in full career on horseback, probably at the gallop, but let them be met by an insurmountable barrier of levelled spears, so that the very last of the troop should feel the opposing shock.

He would likewise have his warriors to remember the evil Scotland had endured from the people of England, and what she might still suffer were they not stayed in their hostile intention. As the matter stood, those beside him had three advantages, which he would enumerate. In the first place, the right was on their side, and God would thereby bestow his favour upon them.

---

1. Bruce, from his long experience in war, knew well how essential it was to success that discipline should be strictly observed in those ranks who were placed front to front with the enemy. We learn from Barbour that, three years after the battle of Bannockburn, the King was in Ireland, and having issued orders that none should quit the ranks, the following incident we give in the language of his biographer:— 'Two English yeomen having discharged their arrows against Sir Colin Campbell, the king's nephew, he rashly rode off, at full speed, to avenge the insult, forgetful of the strict injunctions which had just been issued. The king, highly offended at this flagrant breach of discipline, immediately followed, and struck his nephew so violently with his truncheon, that he was nearly beaten from his horse. 'Such breach of orders,' said the king, 'might occasion the loss of the whole army.'—*Kerr*, vol. ii.

Secondly, the English approached in full dependence of their own power to capture the Scottish people, and brought hither riches in abundance, so that if victory be on the side of Scotland, the poorest of her sons shall share in the spoil. And thirdly, it was for the lives of the brave men around him, for their children, and for their wives, for the liberty and freedom of their own land, that they go into battle, since the foe had come to destroy them, and would have no mercy upon them were they to suffer defeat in the field. It became them, therefore, to set bravery against wrong, whereby he prayed them to be most alert at the commencement of the struggle, and meet the enemy at the first onset so sternly that all their ranks in the rear might be impressed with dread and dismay.

Honour, fame, and wealth, freedom and happiness, would be inherited by them all, did they acquit themselves like men. In order that they might not live in thraldom, they had come with him to do battle for liberty.

Greater suffering could not befall them than to be defeated, for, as the English murdered his brother Nigel, so would they also put those around him and himself to death.[2] Of this, however, he had no fear, for by the prowess and strength of these his adherents, they would, through help from above, overcome the foe, especially as the place they were in afforded ample scope for their own movement, but gave insufficient room to their opponents, while it was so defended by nature that those with him could not possibly be outflanked or surrounded.

He also beseeched them that none, through desire of gain, would attempt either to plunder or take prisoners till the field was clear of enemies, and then the whole spoil would be their own. Were this done, they would undoubtedly be honoured with victory. Further, with judicious foresight, he announced that whoever fell in the struggle, his heirs, however young, should instantly succeed to the inheritance, free of any ward or relief.[3]

And now, he continued, let all prepare and be ready for battle, and may God assist and enable us so to meet our enemy that we may come

---

2. When the castle of Kildrummie surrendered in 1306, 'Nigel, the brother of Bruce, a youth of singular comeliness, was among the captives. He was tried by a special commission at Berwick, condemned, hanged, and afterwards beheaded.'—*Hailes*, vol. ii.

3. The same concession was made by James the Fourth at Twizelhaugh, 23rd August 1513, to the chief men of his army, previous to the Battle of Flodden.—*Scots Acts*.

off victorious from the field![4]

A general and enthusiastic cry arose that every arrangement should be carried out as the king had proposed, and while the English seemed to halt till the arrears of their army came forward, the Scots made preparation to rest, retiring to a wood in the rear, which afforded some slight shelter from the dews of night, keeping watch, at the same time, that no sudden movement of the foe should take place without due notice of their approach.

The church, on this occasion, lent its aid to work on the superstitious impressions of the king and the army. Bruce, it appears, was in possession of the miraculous arm of St. Fillan, and the relic being enclosed in a silver case, the king had it generally borne at the head of his army. But his chaplain, foreseeing the danger to which the Scots were exposed, and having slight faith in their prowess against the English, had left the arm behind him in a secure place, and brought the empty casket, which was placed in the tent of the king. During the night, when the monarch was engaged in his devotions to God and St. Fillan, the lid of the case, it is written, opened of itself, and suddenly closing, the priest exclaimed that a marvel had been wrought, for the arm was there, and that this betokened success to the Scots! (See note following). Bruce, like a wise man, turned this to the best account, and there can be no doubt that he spent the night in anxious thought, wrestling, as it were, to provide in every way for the impending crisis of his fortune on the morrow. In this feeling, and in dependence on the Most High, we may be assured he was cordially seconded by the whole army.

> Note:—'But King Robert all the night before the battell tooke litle rest, having great care in his mind for the suertie of his armie, one while revolving in his consideration this chance, and another while that; yea, and sometimes he fell to devout contemplation, making his praier to God and Saint Phillane, whose arme, as it was set and enclosed in a silver case, he supposed

---

4. The author has not marked the speech of Bruce with points, as if the king had actually uttered it, for though Barbour ascribes it to him, the poetical churchman may have partly embellished it from his own imagination. Still it well merits attention, for human feeling and passion are the same all over the world. In *The Persians* of *Æschylus*, the solemn outburst of patriotism rising from the Greeks, as they moved to the sea-fight of Salamis, may well form a text to the admonition of the Scottish king:—'*Sons of the Greeks, advance! our country free, your children, and your wives, The temples of your fathers' gods, Your fathers' sepulchres—All—all are now at stake.*'

had beene the same time within his tent, trusting the better fortune to follow by presence thereof. In the meane time, as he was thus making his praiers, the case suddenlie opened, and clapped to againe. The king's chapleine being present, astonied therewith, went to where the case stood, and finding the arme within it, he cried to the king and other that were present, how there was a great miracle wrought, confessing that he brought the emptie case to the field, and left the arme at home, least that relike should have beene lost in the field, if any thing chanced to the armie otherwise than well.'—*Hollinshed.* 'Macgregor, who furnished the relic of St. Fillan, which had been preserved on his lands of Strathfillan, is said to have fought bravely at Bannockburn,'—*Nimmo*, vol. i.

Hollinshed, drawing his statement from Boece, says that on the day before the battle, when two knights of Brabant, in the English army, heard many reproachful words spoken of King Robert Bruce, they, disliking such expressions, had the hardihood to observe they wished victory might fall to him. On this being reported to King Edward, he caused them by trumpet to be sent in derision to the Scottish Army, that they might, according to their remarks, render aid to the enemy. He then caused proclamation to be made that whoever brought the heads of these men to him should, by way of recompense, receive one hundred *marks*.

During the night, it is said, a Scotsman, Alexander Seton by name, who was in the English army, deserted, and arriving at the Scottish camp, communicated the intelligence to Bruce that were he to join battle early next morning he would easily overcome the English. The king, however, depended on the security of his position and other circumstances too much to run the hazard of an unorganised attack, and the result proved eminently successful.

But when the English saw and heard how Clifford with his cavalry had been defeated and beaten off by Randolph, how the van under the Earls of Gloucester and Hereford had been driven back, how Robert Bruce had slain Henry de Bohun, a stalwart knight, with his own hand, and how the Scottish Army seemed determined for battle, they were much discomforted, observing among themselves that their chief men led them to the conflict, but that they were to fight in an unjust cause, and that God loved what was right, and would accordingly punish those who were in the wrong. The chief earls and barons of England, on hearing this, caused heralds to proclaim throughout the host that the fighting men were not to be dismayed in any way, but to take courage and behold their great numbers and their prowess, which no enemy was able to withstand. All were also admonished to fight stoutly, thereby maintaining their own honour, and that of England.

King Edward having, with the advice of his nobles, resolved not to commence battle till next morning, the numerous divisions of his troops prepared to rest for the night, several detachments encamping on the spots they occupied, and others descending to the low and fertile grounds, which spread like a carse,[5] and at that time may have been named so, all along the side of Bannockburn. As has been stated, it was now the vigil of St. John, and many in the camp, well knowing the solemn position in which they were placed, must have prepared themselves consistently to take their fortune whatever might befall. Others again, and probably the more numerous class, wearied with the march, and taking advantage of the time, spent the night in drunkenness, revelry, and disorder. In all communities there are reckless men who, though danger be imminent, are bent on enjoying the present hour, and, accordingly, when opportunity occurs, give themselves up to every bodily indulgence. The English camp, therefore, must have presented a very different aspect from that in which the Scots were assembled, waiting to work out their own liberty, and the independence of their fatherland.

---

5. Barbour states how the English harboured down in the carse. The term is now applied to the broad level ground bordering on the Forth, which is upwards of a mile to the north-east from the locality where the army was stationed.

CHAPTER 8

The Armies Confront Each Other

On the morning of Monday, the 24th June 1314, Bruce observed the English Army in the exact position he wished it to be, consequently he drew up his squadrons on the ground he had selected for battle. Having signified his wish that the brave warriors before him should receive the sacrament, Maurice, Abbot of Inchaffray, in Strathearn, Perthshire, who accompanied the king, performed mass on an eminence in front of the Scottish Army, desiring all to confess their sins and supplicate God on behalf of their country.[1] The troops then partook of breakfast, which partly consisted of bread and wine,[2] and then deliberately made themselves ready for the struggle.

Next, they took their places under their respective banners, which we may suppose streamed brightly in the morning breeze. Bruce, in the company of his leading men, proceeded, according to the custom before battle at that time, to confer knighthood on Walter Steward, James Douglas, and other gallant warriors, who were deserving of such honour, each being promoted according to his degree. Then each division went forward and occupied the place assigned to it, filling up the line of battle as arranged by the king, and the whole extended from the hollow, north of Halbert's Bog, upwards to the south-west on the high ground, near the bend of the Bannock above Park Mill.[3]

1. On the morow, he gaderit al his army to messe to ressave the body of God, to mak thaim have the more curage aganis thair ennimes. In this army wes ane devoit man, named Maritius, Abbot of Inchechaffray, quhilk said messe on ane hie mote, and ministerit the Eucharist to the king and his nobillis; and causit his preistis to mak ministratioun thairof to the residew of the army.—*Bellenden*, vol, ii.
2. Bruce refreshed his troops with bread and wine.—Turner vol. ii.
3. In the large map completed by the Board of Ordnance, the site of the battle is marked close to the south-east side of the road between Coxet Hill and Graystale. The author is not a military man, but from a most careful, (continued next page),

Retaining possession of this place, while the thoroughfares at Milton and below Brock's Brae were rendered impassable, the Scots could not be outflanked, and hence the English must of necessity be compelled to meet them here in battle. We know not where the trees grew that were near or among the various lines of troops, but portions of wood arose over the whole neighbourhood. Nor do we believe that the entire army was collected together in these several divisions. They might be completed, so far as numbers could be made up, but considerable detachments were doubtless stationed above Milton, or near the Bore-stone, on Coxet Hill, and beyond the extremity of the right wing, at a short distance from Graystale. These were to watch the progress of the contest, and in case any party quitted the main body of the foe and made an advance, the said Scots were to meet and repel them, or at least to convey intimation of the circumstance to the king.

It has been already stated that, according to the direction of Bruce, the Scottish Army was to be separated into four divisions, and how the charge of the right wing devolved upon Edward Bruce. The van at first was intended to be led by Randolph, but Bruce, on surveying the ground, would seem to have altered his original plan, for the highest part of the front lines was where his brother was placed, and this point, he well knew, would be first assailed by the enemy. Accordingly, the body of above seven thousand warriors, under Sir Edward Bruce, came to form the van of the Scots, for they were before the others, who were stationed somewhat behind, on lower ground, and their heroic leader had the angle of the stream already mentioned, hid far down among trees, on his right hand.

Next to him, on his left, but a little to the rear, with a space between the divisions, so narrow as not to allow a passage for the English horse, was Randolph, Earl of Moray, leading a like number of men; and still farther to the north-east, slightly to the rear, also on the lower ground, and near to the head of Halbert's Bog, stood Sir Walter Steward and Sir James Douglas, completing with their spearmen, equal in number to the others, the whole front lines of battle.[4] Taking into account the

---

inspection of the battlefield, taking into account all the circumstances connected with it, he is of opinion that the front line of battle, presented at first by the Scots to the enemy, must have been nearly two hundred yards farther to the south. This gave Robert Bruce, from the highest point of the rise directly north of Park Mill, a full view of the whole field, and any impartial man must perceive how necessary this was to the king in regulating every impending movement of his forces.

4. These divisions, be it remembered, were drawn up, as we gather from Barbour, somewhat obliquely, the rear corner to the left of that led by, (continued next page),

spaces which separated these divisions, each section would average about fourteen men deep, a force that, judiciously guided, would, if they fought well, accomplish much on a stricken field.

Again, on the highest ground beside, or rather behind. Sir Edward Bruce and Randolph, with the fourth division in reserve, the king was stationed on horseback, regulating the whole, and watching attentively from his lofty position every movement, both of his own troops and those of the enemy. Apart from these four bodies of warriors were the five hundred cavalry, who had overcome Clifford, led by Sir Robert Keith, hereditary Marshal of Scotland. Moreover, a considerable band of archers, of whom we are unable to state the number, were placed probably near the openings of the several divisions, but, on account of the rise of the ground, somewhat near to that of Sir Edward Bruce. At this instant both armies must have presented a stirring and most magnificent sight. Before the king were his own devoted subjects, ready to offer up their lives for the freedom of Scotland; and from the stream of Bannock, mile beyond mile, south-east to the hill of Plean, shaded occasionally by patches of the forest, but covering the whole side of the declivity which sloped down towards the brook, one enormous crowd appeared of men, horses, and carriages.

The latter were stationed more in the distance, but in front and behind, up to and beyond Foot o' Green, were banners, flags, and pennons, of every colour, waving beyond each other in the breeze, while armour, shields, helmets, morions, and weapons, glanced and sparkled above the bearers far and wide. Earls, knights, and bannerets on horseback, gorgeously decorated in their surcoats of various bright hues, seemed innumerable, while squires, cavalry, and infantry, comprising spearmen and archers, densely mingled together, filled up every available space of ground. Their immense numbers scarcely allowed of any opening between them, and we may readily conclude that no exhibition of martial pomp and grandeur to an equal extent was ever witnessed in this land. Fancy delights to contemplate the gorgeous display, and we may conceive how it thrilled the heart of Bruce, and awakened feelings of awe and sublimity in the bosoms, not only of his noble adherents, but of many a brave Scottish peasant.

Ere the English moved forward, several of the leading men of mature age, knowing how the greater part of the army, by watching and

---

Sir Edward Bruce approaching the front comer to the right of the men under Randolph, and the left rear of his warriors nearing the right front of those headed by the Steward and Douglas.

revelry through the night, had enjoyed little or no sleep, endeavoured to prevail with the king to defer the conflict till the following day, but the younger chiefs derided such counsel, and the prudence of the former was set aside. The Earl of Gloucester advocated delay, and the king foolishly called him a traitor for his discretion. The taunt was indignantly repelled by the remark that before the day was over proof would be given he was neither traitor nor coward. It was some time ere the arrangements for commencing the attack were completed, and thus the leaders lingered that they might receive orders to advance.

Meantime King Edward was accompanied by Aymer de Valence, Earl of Pembroke, on one side of his bridle, and Sir Giles de Argentine, one of the bravest knights in Europe, at the other, also bishops and ecclesiastics who kept near to him, together with five hundred armed horsemen as his bodyguard. It would appear he was stationed somewhere in the neighbourhood of Chartershall Mains, and when gazing northward, on observing the Scottish army drawn up in hostile array, all on foot, he was somewhat amazed at the sight. Looking at the enormous numbers of his own forces, he considered they must be invincible in battle, wherever and whenever it took place; nor did it even enter his mind either to lead them on under superior generalship, or cause them to meet the enemy upon suitable ground, in order to come off victorious. Believing, therefore, that Bruce's army would not dare to oppose him, he inquired of Sir Ingram de Umfreville, who knew them well, 'If yonder Scots would presume to fight?'

'Yea, surely, sire,' said the knight, 'and it is the most fearful sight I ever beheld, when they are resolved to do battle against the whole force of England. Truly I know the people, and if your Majesty would please to follow my advice, I can devise how they may easily be overcome. Let us withdraw the army and retreat, as if for fear, beyond our baggage and pavilions, on our way to England, and the desire of spoil shall so work upon them that no captain may keep them together, and thus, when their ranks are broken, we shall secure an easy victory.'

'I will not assent to this,' said the king, 'nor will I turn from doing battle with such a low, despicable concourse of people.' By this time the Abbot of Inchaffray, who had previously celebrated mass, now advanced, walking bare-footed along the front of the Scottish lines as they stood prepared for the onset, and carrying a cross wherein a crucifix was suspended, he raised it as a banner,[5] and admonished his

---

5. Maritius, the abbot forsaid, tuke the croce, in quhilk the crucifix wes hinging, and ereckit it afore the army in maner of ane baner.—Bellenden, vol ii.

countrymen in most earnest and appropriate words to perform their duty nobly in so righteous and glorious a cause.[6] When he had done this, the whole army knelt down, and confessing their shortcomings, put up a brief but fervent prayer that the Almighty would remember them in mercy, and crown their efforts with success.

When all the divisions of the Scots thus knelt down, King Edward, who beheld them, believed they were supplicating for pardon, and turning again to Umfreville, observed, 'These people dare not encounter us in the field—see they all kneel to us for mercy!'

'They do seek for mercy, my liege,' said the knight, 'but not from your Majesty. They implore Heaven for pardon and for help in the struggle, and believe me, sire, these men will either win or die where they stand, nor will they fly for all the power England can bring against them.'

'Be it so, then,' said the king, and almost immediately after the trumpets sounded the onset of battle.

---

6. The abbat of Inchchafiraie, aforesaid, came forth before the battels, with the crucifix in his hands, bearing it aloft like a standard, admonishing them valiantlie to take in hand the defence of their countrie and the libertie of their posteritie; for, saith he, you must not euerie man fight as it were for his own privat defence, his own house and children, but euerie man for all men, and all men for euerie man, must fight for the libertie, life, patrimonie, children, and wines of all the realme; for such and so great is the dignitie of our countrie as they which deface or spoile are to be punished with perpetuall fier, and they which doo preserve it are to be recompensed with an eternal crowne of glorie.'—*Hollinshed.*

CHAPTER 9

The Battle Commences

Scotia's bard has given us an animated *Address of Bruce to his Army* in a measure to suit the old stirring tune, which tradition sanctions as the 'March' of the patriot on the present occasion. Rude war-pipes or horns might give forth awakening notes to thrill the bosoms of the Scots, but that the ranks moved forward we consider very doubtful. It is more probable that, like the rocks of their own sea-girt land, they firmly awaited the approach of their foes only to dash them back like ocean waves broken in a boisterous storm. The van of the English, consisting of armed men and horse under the Earls of Gloucester and Hereford, flanked on the left by the archers, held on up the slope, direct to the foremost Scottish division, headed by Sir Edward Bruce;[1] and it seems probable they charged at the quick trot or gallop, with great fury. Owing, however, to a dispute between the leaders, and to the consequent irregularity of the movement, the English being partly broken, made little or no impression on the Scottish lines, though several on both sides were slain.[2]

---

1. Moore blames the English cavalry for beginning the struggle while the sun was shining on their gilt shields and burnished helms, instead of waiting till noon. See also *Meyrick*, vol. i., and Turner , vol. ii.. This is clearly a mistake, for the sun rose to the right of the English in the morning, he shone on their backs towards noon, and was descending on their left to the west when the Scots gained the victory.
2. The English van, led by Gloucester and Hereford, now spurred forward their horses, and at full gallop charged the right wing of the Scots, commanded by Edward Bruce; but a dispute as to precedence cau.sed the charge, though rapid, to be broken and irregular. Gloucester, who had been irritated the day before by some galling remarks of the king, insisted on leading the van, a post which of right belonged to Hereford as Constable of England. To this Hereford would not agree; and Gloucester, as they disputed, seeing the Scottish right advancing, sprang forward at the head of his own division, and, without being, (continued next page),

The cause why the division of Sir Edward Bruce was first encountered might be that this body occupied, as has been stated, the highest ground on the battlefield, that it was in advance of the other divisions, and that the attack could be made more effectual on this point from the shield borne on the left arm of the Scottish soldier, leaving the right side more exposed to the sword or spear. All this King Robert seems to have foreseen, and made his arrangements accordingly. Here also we may perceive how the English archers knowingly flanked the left of the van, and thereby obtained the loftiest position, whence their shafts might fly with more deadly aim against the Scots.

The shock was tremendous, for the men-at-arms rushed onward as if to break through the serried barrier of spears, probably two or three yards broad; [3] and though some of the Scots were borne to the earth, many of their assailants were overthrown. The horses which were pierced plunged wildly, and their riders falling, were either trampled upon by others, or when a slight advance was made, they were struck to death by the Scottish axes.

At every onset the crash of broken spears might be heard at a great distance. Still the Scots stood firm as onward came the cavalry without ceasing, while the English archers, who were distant nearly twelve score yards, poured incessantly into the dense masses of the opposing spearmen their showers of arrows, each about three feet long. Some of the English chroniclers say that several of these fell short of their aim, and pierced the undefended backs of their own people.[4] The latter, who were on horseback, would more readily intercept the flight of these shafts when aimed at the Scots, whose front lines were all on foot.

---

supported by the rest of the van, attacked the enemy, who received them with a shock which caused the meeting of their spears to be heard a great way off, and threw many knights from their saddles whose horses were stabbed and rendered furious by their wounds.'—Tytler, vol. i.

3. Bruce compacted his men into a thick mass, a bristled hedge, like the Macedonian *phalanx*, which from its union and solidity was impenetrable.—Turner, vol. ii. Before the battle of Arbela, Alexander formed his men sixteen deep, and placed in their grasp the *sarissa*, as the Macedonian pike was called, and which was twenty-four feet in length, and when couched for action reached eighteen feet in front of the soldier; so that, as a space of two feet was allowed between the ranks, the spears of the five files behind him projected in front of each front-rank man.'—Creasy, vol. i.; Grote, vol. viii.

4. When they shot right forth they slew fewe of the Scots by reason of their armed breasts, but many of the Englishmen by reason of their naked backs.—*Moore*, quoted by Stowe.

The remaining divisions of the English, who were compressed together as if they formed one column of enormous length and breadth, began partly to deploy on crossing the Bannock, and advancing upwards to the field, threw themselves in succession headlong upon the foe.

That body of the Scots under the command of the redoubted Randolph, who were stationed near those already fighting that the latter might not be taken in flank, met the assailants in line, and maintained their ground gallantly, repelling the horsemen and foot with the same bravery as their fellow-warriors to the right had shown. The encounter was not less fierce than before, for not a foot were the Scots driven back, but they rather advanced, treading over every obstacle in their way.

Besides, they adhered strictly to the command of the king, for they kept closely, shoulder to shoulder, in the line of battle. The array was never broken, but amid the dreadful struggle of man opposed to man, inflicting on each other wounds and death, the Scots, as they pressed forward, seemed plunged in a stormy sea covered with men, horses, and weapons of every kind, which were wielded with tremendous energy.

Blood flowed in every direction, and the Scots, though opposed to such overwhelming numbers, still bore onward, the English encountering them most fiercely, and doing all in their power to check the course of these intrepid northern warriors.

The massive columns of English, still pressing onward to the right, came at length into battle with the troops under Sir Walter Steward and Sir James Douglas, who kept near to the division of Randolph and still preserved the front of the Scottish lines unbroken. A similar onslaught was made by the enemy with still greater vehemence, if possible, in order to break through the opposing Scottish spears, and again the English, both horse and foot, were repelled with the most determined resolution.

Steed after steed was thrown down, and knight, squire, and man-at-arms on the side of England fell, yet their places were instantly occupied by the masses behind, and the battle on the whole line became more fierce and terrible. The soil was covered with the dead and the dying, while the struggling combatants waded through coagulated streams of blood, yet no lapse took place in the stem valour everywhere displayed, and the Scots, advancing as they fought, trode over prostrate horse and man as if all opposition was in vain.

While the armies thus opposed each other in direful conflict, Robert Bruce observed how the shafts from the English bows were telling most fatally on the right wing of his army, especially among his own archers, who were not clothed like the spearmen in defensive armour. For this he was prepared, and giving orders that Sir Robert Keith, Earl Marshal, should lead the troop of five hundred horse under his command against these bowmen, the movement was at once accomplished. Threading their way probably amid the furze and trees that grew on the north-east bank of the Bannock above Park Mill, they outflanked the English cavalry, and, without the slightest opposition, fell on the unarmed men, who were lightly clad and altogether unprotected, for the attention of King Edward and his nobles must at the time have been directed intensely towards the main front of the battle.

A brief space elapsed ere Keith, Earl Marshal accomplished his mission, but ultimately the English archers were totally defeated. Many were borne to the ground or killed, while those who fled were almost unable, from the pressure, to obtain room among the English troops, hence, during the latter part of the day, they never rallied to afford any especial assistance to their countrymen.

Meanwhile, the Scottish archers, though not very expert with the bow, being armed with swords, knives, and battle-axes, now that the shower of steel from their opponents had ceased, came forward and aimed their shafts with most fatal effect on the enemy.

When Robert Bruce saw Keith, Earl Marshal return after dispersing the English archers, and also observing before him his three divisions still making way on the enemy, maintaining their squares in line with each other, and fighting most bravely, he was, apart from the excitement, much gratified, for every movement indicated a prosperous result. Addressing the chief men near him who headed his own division ere they joined in battle, he cheered them with words of encouragement, desiring they also should acquit themselves most gallantly, so that any opposing force might be unable to withstand their onset.

The several oblong squares before him were fighting most fiercely, and had so gallantly encountered the foe, that were the latter pressed something more they would doubtless be overcome. 'Now then,' he is reported to have said to the leaders in his own division, 'let us go forward, and support our fellow-countrymen in their glorious cause, for we trust we shall have assistance from on high to punish these assailants as they deserve.'

On this being said they advanced chiefly to the right, filling up the weakest portions of the lines, and taking their place where the battle was most fiercely disputed.[5]

---

5. It would seem from some expressions in Barbour that the King of Scots brought up the reserve to the right of his army. This shows that there had been a great slaughter of the Scots, by which, hi that circumscribed ground, there was place left for the reserve to fall into the line.—*Hailes*, vol. ii. This is every way probable, for Sir Edward Bruce not only withstood the first onset of the English, but sustained it to the last, and being on the highest ground, the strength of the enemy, we may be certain, was chiefly directed to this quarter, which seems to have been all foreseen, and provided for by Bruce.

Chapter 10

Battle Continued

The whole martial forces of Scotland, except the slight detachments near them in reserve, were now engaged in the fight, so that the ground, from the high banks of the Bannock, north of Park Mill, to the head of Halbert's Bog, and down southward to the Bannock again, was crowded with fighting men, while, in the opposing lines of conflict, each was struggling between life and death for victory. Again and again did the mailed chivalry of England, in heavy masses, attempt to break through the opposing barrier of pointed steel, and as often did they fail, nor could they possibly draw back, for those behind, closely wedged together, would allow of no retreating, and, thus environed on each side, they fell pierced with wounds. Horses sprang away with empty saddles, adding to the general tumult and dismay, while others rolled over with men upon them in mailed armour, who, being unable to rise, were trodden to the earth in helpless confusion.

All this time the Scottish archers, winging their shafts where they fell most effectually, performed gallant service; nor did they constantly use the bow, for as occasion served they seized their axes, and so handled them that neither helm nor habergeon could ward off the stroke. It was a fearful struggle, for the whole Scottish front, moving still onward, forced their way, as our national poet says, 'red-wat shod' over every obstacle of men and horses, dead or dying. Nor did the opposite lines of the English seem to slacken in any degree, for everywhere they appeared in countless numbers, taking the place, whenever it occurred, of those who fell, and endeavouring, with determined energy, to break the overwhelming rush of spears, that a gap might be made whereby the cavalry might enter and bear to earth the undaunted Scots. The latter truly could not maintain their progress unscathed, for many a steady spearman fell, yielding up his breath in stem defence of the liberties of his native land.

Barbour himself soars into the region of poetry on describing the scene, appealing to the great Ruler of the universe, while he writes how Sir Edward Bruce and his gallant warriors acquitted themselves in the fight so nobly that their shock of spears was tremendous, and that the Scots maintained themselves in such a compact body that whoever fell before them never had the power to rise again. Many gallant feats were performed, and many a brave man killed, for the field was red with gore, while surcoats, clothing, and various appendages to garments of brilliant appearance were so stained with soil and blood they could not be known. In the same way our venerable chronicler delineates with a skilful hand how the Steward and Douglas, with their power, so pressed the enemy that whoever witnessed it might well say these heroes were worthy of all honour, while many a splendid horse plunged back amid the throng without its rider.

Then he alludes to Randolph, telling how he and his devoted soldiers made their way wherever they came, repelling at every step the mailed, courageous, and high-minded chivalry of England. Here and there also, between the divisions of spearmen, the archers plied their bows so incessantly during the desperate struggle of both man and horse, who were only a few yards from them, that almost every arrow flew to its aim, and every axe dealt an irresistible blow. Moreover, the whole front of the Scots, obedient to the strict injunction of the king, was maintained in regular line, for no opening could be made among them, and the English were either slain or driven backward, surely, though at times slowly, yet ever retreating.

This desperate fighting continued for a considerable time, while Robert Bruce observed that assistance was promptly rendered wherever it was required. Accordingly, the English, finding it impossible to make way against the enemy, were amazed, and at length they hesitated to renew the heavy and repeated charges they made at first to break through or circumvent the Scots. This slackness was at once observed by the latter, and among them the cry arose, which soon circulated along the whole lines—'On them, on them!—they fail, they fail!' Every Scotsman thereby felt his heart animated afresh, and in front of the several divisions the assault was sustained with the most desperate energy and enthusiasm. The important event which would echo over Britain for a thousand years was about to be decided, victory on the one side and defeat on the other was imminent, for another hour would in all likelihood determine the problem.

While the battle continued to be struck thus fiercely, the number of camp followers, or gillies, meaning the male servants, and numbering above fifteen thousand, who were sent away from the army, as has been stated, to a hollow north of Graystale, on Gillies Hill, had watched the struggle most attentively from the higher ground, and as they observed their countrymen not only confronting the English in unbroken lines, but repelling and bearing them backward, they resolved, in accordance we believe with what had been previously arranged by the king, to perform a movement which ultimately was most successful.[1]

Selecting among themselves the man or men deputed by Bruce to direct them, for an office of that kind regularly falls to the most skilful, they gathered together all the poles and straight young trees stript of branches they could procure, and fastening to the upper end of each either a sheet or a piece of coloured linen, such as could be supplied, for the spare clothing of the army was there, they formed themselves into ranks and columns, and, appearing in hostile array, came marching over the edge of the hill, sounding their horns in wild clamour, directly down to the battlefield. Except for some natural trees or bushes, as there were scarcely any undulations of the ground, the whole course of their progress was observed by every opposing Englishman not engaged in actual conflict, and the sight apparently of a fresh and powerful army hastening to assist the Scots, spread dismay and terror everywhere among them.

On approaching the throng of battle, the gillies shouted to the full extent of their voices, 'Slay, slay! upon them hastily!' and the struggle became more and more deadly. By this time the English, who had fought face to face with the Scots from the commencement of the battle till now, were driven down towards the Bannock, yet they preserved their front manfully, dealing their blows, as if through despair, with tremendous effect, while behind, their fellow-countrymen were still so massed together that no space was left for retreat.

On seeing the accession, however, of numbers to the Scottish ranks, astonishment and fear began to unnerve their resolution, while the gillies seized such weapons as were at hand, or could be caught from the dead and dying around them, and, uniting with the infantry, struck

1. At a distance, in a valley, lay fifteen thousand followers of the army, whom the king dared not bring into the field, but whom he instructed to show themselves in the heat of the conflict as a new army hastening to the aid of their countrymen,'— *Lingard*, vol. iii.

down whoever of their opponents they could reach. The Scottish cavalry began now to perform a most important part, for whenever an opening occurred in the ranks of the English, these horsemen pressed forward among them, and made immense slaughter.

About this time the Earl of Gloucester, in an attempt to turn the tide of battle, rode fiercely upon the advancing Scots, and, without being duly supported by his own followers, fell, pierced by the Scottish spears. Bruce now perceiving how the ranks of the enemy were giving way, raised his war cry, and all those who were with him, animated by the prospect of victory, united with all their might in dealing destruction upon the reeling crowds before them. During the whole period that the English were driven back, till the stream was reached, and even then, from the site of Park Mill to that of Chartershall, a series of desperate encounters would appear to have taken place. Barbour observes the Bannock was so bridged over with drowned horses and men that they who wished to cross it might have done so dry-footed. [2] At last, confounded, or overcome with alarm, terror, and amazement, whole squadrons of the English now betook themselves to flight. The battle was at length won, Scotland had conquered, and England was compelled to suffer an ignominious defeat.

---

2. We question the accuracy of this statement in one point only, for whether man or beast be drowned, they are generally found in deep water; hence, if the stream was so choked up, it must have been by men and horses who were killed and not drowned.

CHAPTER 11

Flight of the English

We may readily conceive the astonishment and agonising feelings at this time of the English King. It is said that on the crisis of the fight, when the Scots were likely to win, he attempted to ride forward with or without his body guard, that he might dye his steel in the blood of the Scots;[1] but it is more likely he was held back by those around him; and when at last De Valence, Earl of Pembroke, saw that the chance of victory was over and danger at hand, he seized the king's bridle and led him unwillingly away from the sickening scene. Sir Giles de Argentine, true to his trust, whose lofty conception of knightly honour would not allow him to depart a fugitive from a stricken field, accompanied the monarch till he thought him safely away from danger, and then observing it was not his wont to fly from battle, wished him, 'God speed!'

Turning his horse again to the field, he spurred forward, and shouting his war cry, 'An Argentine! An Argentine!' he encountered several horsemen and the infantry under Sir Edward Bruce, where he gallantly fell as became a brave and heroic knight. His loss was deplored by the Scots as well as the English, for he was accounted the third best knight in Christendom.

Panic-struck at the terrible calamity, and scarcely knowing what to do or where to go, the King of England, accompanied by his bishops, and having five hundred of his principal nobility around him,[2] rode

---

1. Could we attach credit to the words of Patrick Gordon, King Edward rushed into the throng, and fought with the bravery which characterised his race, for he killed the Earl of Strathearn and his son, beside other knights whose names are not recorded.
2. Hugh de Lespencer, 'that cowardly bird of prey,' as Hailes calls him, quoting from Moore, was also of the number.

at last direct to Stirling, by the nearest approach, and ascending to the castle, sought instant admittance. Sir Philip Mowbray observed the fortress was at his monarch's will, but if he came within, he would undoubtedly be taken prisoner, for none in all England could either rescue him or render help. Whereupon he advised him to retain his knights by him, and wind round beneath the Park, so as to get away from the strife, in which case none would be able to do him injury. Hereupon he departed, taking his way beneath the castle, past the Round Table, and below the east side of the Park, on the direct road to Linlithgow, with the utmost speed. Sir James Douglas, who perceived his flight, besought King Robert to allow him to give chase, which was granted, but as large numbers of the English were still near, no more than about sixty mounted horsemen could be spared for the pursuit.[3]

When King Edward quitted the field, and the royal banner of England was borne away, any resistance on the side of her sons was hopeless, and, depressed by the awful calamity which was imminent, each man endeavoured to fly for safety, so that an incredible number were slain. Of those who remained longest on the field the slaughter was immense, for, being without the slightest means of resistance, they were stricken down and destroyed on every side. But parties of the Scots intent on plunder, instead of chasing the enemy, preferred to gather spoil wherever it could be found, and they rifled the slain, besides collecting what booty they could acquire in the English camp, thereby allowing numbers to escape.[4] Many men of rank, as a means of safety, threw off their surcoats and armour, whereby their speed should be increased, and they would not attract attention, and fled half naked over the country in the direction of England.

A large body of the fugitives, who had kept together, after they passed the spot where Bannockburn House now stands, made an attempt to check the pursuers, but without avail, and the place where it is said they all fell is still known in the locality by the name of the 'Bloody Faulds.' Other companies, diverging from the line wherein the pursuit was chiefly made, and, hastening down to the carse, en-

3. Lord Hailes agrees with Barbour as to the number of horsemen with which Douglas gave chase to the fugitives, though Buchanan and Hollinshed increase it to four hundred.

4. Very few of the flying army would have escaped with life and liberty if many of the Scotch soldiers had not preferred the plunder of the English camp (where they found an immense booty) to the pursuit of their enemies.—*Mon. Malms*, quoted by Henry, vol. vii.

deavoured to cross the Forth, in which many of them were drowned. It has been already stated that Bannockburn at that time, below Chartershall, ran deeply amid slake and earth, so that many who lingered on the field, and had escaped slaughter by the lower orders of the Scots, were also overwhelmed in the sluggish stream.[5]

Among the English nobility who fled and were not of the number who accompanied the king, was the Earl of Hereford, who took a southern direction, with many of his followers, and knowing the country, went direct to the castle of Bothwell, which was held by his own countryman, Sir Walter Gilbertson, who took him in over the walls, with fifty of his dependants. The remainder of the fugitives escaped towards England, but only about a fourth of the number reached the Border land in safety, the others being either killed or made prisoners. Another large company who attempted to escape by flight were Welchmen who had accompanied Maurice de Berkeley, but being almost naked, for they wore light linen covering only, many were captured, and still more slain.

Of those who were left with life, and knowing that no mercy would be shown them in flying towards Falkirk, the chief portion— and a large number they were—sought their way northward, and took refuge on and around the crags to the west and north of Stirling Castle, and almost covered these rocky precipices. Indeed, with other fugitives, they were so numerous that King Robert entertained some doubt they might rally again, wherefore he kept his good men near him to repress any assault, for which cause he could not afford Douglas a sufficient number of horse to pursue King Edward, and accordingly the latter got safely away.

One may conceive the consternation of those men, women, and youths, who were left with the provision-waggons, etc., when they beheld their monarch with his nobles flying past them on horseback at full speed for life. Mile after mile this must have been the case, and the sight would indicate to them the hard fate they would probably have to undergo ere they could hope to set foot upon their own land. It was a most exciting chase. While Sir James Douglas was pursuing King Edward past the Torwood he met Sir Lawrence Abernethy with twenty horsemen, who had come with the intention of assisting the

---

5. The channel of the Bannock, ere it enters the valley below Milton, has been deepened considerably since the time of the battle. There is now, and has been for a lengthened period, a gradual descent in its course, for the bridge which spans the stream, near the above village, has been widened on two several occasions.

English, but on observing the result of the battle he swore to be leal and true to Bruce, and joined Douglas in the pursuit.

On passing Linlithgow the Scottish horse approached the fugitives so near that they might almost have come into conflict, but the latter were so numerous that the pursuers deemed it imprudent to stay them in their flight. Keeping, however, close upon them, they watched their chance; and when any one of the English lingered or was left behind, even a short way, he was certain to be either killed or made prisoner. King Edward, aware of his danger, vowed to God or the Virgin that if he might escape with life he would build a house to the Carmelite or White Friars, in which he would place twenty-four brethren; and, in fulfilment of this promise, though in opposition to the advice of one of his parasites, the younger Spencer, Oriel College in Oxford, was erected.

At Winchburgh, a small village eleven miles west of Edinburgh, the English halted to feed their horses, and the pursuers did the same, but, speedily mounting, the former pursued their way direct to the castle of Dunbar, where King Edward and fifteen earls in his company were received by Patrick Dunbar, Earl of March, leaving their horses behind them, which were immediately seized by the Scots. The remainder of the English held onward towards Berwick, but as they were numerous, preserving their array and threatening defiance in case of interruption, Douglas found it necessary to allow them to depart. It is said he left a party of horsemen to capture the king in case he should venture by land to his own kingdom. But when King Edward recovered from his bodily fatigue, his friend and host, the Earl of March,[6] taking from him a release of his service, got him conveyed in a boat, with a few of his chief men, by sea from Dunbar, either to Berwick or Bambrough, which he reached in safety.[7]

---

6. This release, with other documents of Scottish History, Hardyng says, he afterwards delivered into the treasury of King Henry the Fifth, at Boys Vincent, in France, for which he received the manor or villa of Godyngton in Oxfordshire, and which subsequently came into possession of the queen.

7. Barbour says he went in 'a bate be se to Bawmbxirgh,' while Turner observes that, 'getting into a ship, he sailed precipitately to Berwick.'

CHAPTER 12

Liberal Treatment of Prisoners

In relating the above incidents subsequent to the battle, we are impressed with the apparent lack of precaution on the part of King Edward, his advisers, and the English nobility, to whose charge the expedition to Scotland was entrusted. Blindly confiding in their own strength, and deeming that every obstacle would give way before them, no arrangement whatever seems to have been made either to ward off danger or provide for safety in the event of defeat. When the Scots gained the battle, had the English, who were under arms, withdrawn from the field, and kept together in regular order, presenting a barrier of defence, and retreating as well as they could in front of their pursuers, conveying the most valuable portion of their provision and baggage with them, how different had the result been, as to the loss of both life and property. Whenever King Edward quitted the field, the whole remaining divisions of the army who fought for him, being altogether undefended, fled, and were captured, or cut down without mercy, whereas large numbers, under more prudent guidance, might, unscathed, have reached England, and lived to a good old age.

When the battle was decided, and the English who were unwounded and at liberty had left the field, the Scots forthwith commenced to seize upon such spoil as they could secure. Many, indeed, who had previously endured much privation, acquired vast wealth, which enabled them to assume a high station during the remainder of their lives. The king, in the meantime, having sent a goodly battalion of armed men to secure the large number of English who had fled to the crags at Stirling Castle, they speedily accomplished the object of their mission, and made them prisoners. On returning they were also allowed to join the others in plundering the slain, which they did, stripping the bodies, and many secured much spoil. It was a marvellous sight to behold the vast multitude of those who had fallen, for, of our ancient English families, it is presumed that scarcely one could be named who had not an ancestor either killed or made prisoner in the battle, or in the flight from that fatal field.[1]

We believe the exact number of the English who were slain on the field and in flight, and those who were taken prisoners, cannot possibly be ascertained. Following our best authorities, we would say that about thirty thousand were slain in battle, and fell as fugitives on the way to their own country. Nearly five hundred of the chief men accompanied the king and escaped, but about two hundred knights were killed on the field and seven hundred esquires. Taking the above statement as approximating to the truth, while King Edward brought one hundred thousand men to the field, allowing for a few thousands of prisoners, something less than sixty-five thousand would get away with life, and this may be near an average of what has occurred, with regard to numbers only, in very many battles from the earliest date to the present time. The servants and camp-followers are not comprised in this statement. Many of these undoubtedly would be killed, while others would be fortunate enough to escape.

Among the nobles who were killed, the most illustrious was Gilbert de Clare, Earl of Gloucester. He was nephew to the king, his mother being Joan of Acre, daughter to Edward the First. When the ranks of the English gave way towards the close of the battle, Gloucester as has been said, spurred forward against the Scots, and not being duly supported by his train of five hundred men-at-arms, a few of whom might have rescued him, he was instantly dismounted and slain. King Robert Bruce being related to the earl,[2] mourned in secret for his death, and causing his body to be conveyed to a neighbouring church, it was waked there all the night. Sir Robert Clifford, another gallant warrior, who encountered Randolph previous to the battle, but without success, was also found among the slain.

The same honour was bestowed on his remains that was awarded to the Earl of Gloucester, and both bodies, free of any ransom, were

---

1. If the list (of the slain and those made prisoners, as supplied by the continuator of Trivet's *Annals*) were complete, most of the English families would find the names of their predecessors among the slain, or among the prisoners at Bannockburn.— *Hailes*, Note, vol. ii.

2. His grandfather, Robert, the competitor for the crown, married Isabel, daughter of Gilbert de Clare, seventh Earl of Gloucester, consequently she was his grandmother.—*Banks*, vol. i.

sent to King Edward at Berwick, to be interred in England with the honours due to their birth and valour. Among others. Lord William le Mareshall had also fallen, and Sir Edmund de Mauley, High Steward of England, was discovered drowned in Bannockburn. Of the other men of rank who fell, the attentive reader is referred to the appendix, where a number of names are recorded.[3]

On the side of Scotland the loss of men must also have been considerable, for it is probable the Scottish chroniclers, who state the number to be about four thousand, intentionally kept the figure low.[4] Of the chief men, only two were killed, Sir William Vipont and Sir Walter Ross. The latter seems to have been an especial favourite with Sir Edward Bruce, who made much lamentation when he heard of his death.[5] When, however, the battle was honourably won. King Robert and his company were most joyful on the occasion, being highly delighted at their good fortune. They thanked God that of his grace He had enabled them to preserve in their own land all they held hallowed and dear, and, as they required rest, after every arrangement for safety had been completed, they accordingly withdrew, each to the place where he might enjoy repose.

Next morning early, as King Robert went forth to survey the battlefield, an English knight. Sir Marmaduke Twenge,[6] who, at the close of the conflict seeing no chance of escape, had hid himself amid some bushes, came forward, and bending on his knee, presented himself before Bruce. The king knew him at once, and giving him welcome, asked to whom he was prisoner.

'To none, save to your Majesty,' said the knight.

'Then I receive you,' observed Bruce, and forthwith treated him with much courtesy. He dwelt with the king for a time, and the latter not only sent him to England free of ransom but bestowed upon him handsome gifts. Moreover, Sir Philip Mowbray also sought the king,

---

3. See Appendix Note C.

4. Hollinshed mentions that about four thousand fell.

5. Some improper intimacy would appear to have existed between Sir Edward Bruce and Isabella, sister of Ross, but the story is not clearly authenticated. Sir Edward married the sister of David de Strathbogie, Earl of Athole, whom, it is said, he slighted; and her brother, in revenge for the deed, assaulted the king's headquarters at Cambuskenneth, when the two armies were about to engage, and slew the guard with the commander Sir William Keith. In 1317 Athole went over to the service of England, and in 1323 a sentence of forfeiture was issued against him.—Kerr, vol. i.

6. He was a noted warrior, having conducted himself most gallantly against Wallace in the Battle of Stirling.

and yielding to him the castle of Stirling, entered into an agreement to serve him in the capacity of a true subject, which he performed faithfully to the end of his life. It also occurred that Ralph de Monthermer, who had married Joan of Acre, mother to the Earl of Gloucester, fled along with the king on his way to Dunbar, but, falling behind, was taken prisoner.

He bore the target, or, as Stow calls it, the 'the shield or scale,' belonging to King Edward, but when he was brought before Bruce, from the accidental familiarity which once existed between them at the court of England, he, according to Dugdale, 'was pardoned his fine for redemption,[7] who thereupon returned into England, and brought the king's target which had been taken in that fight, but prohibited the use thereof.'

Roger de Northburge, keeper of the king's signet, and his two clerks, Roger de Wikenfelde and Thomas de Switon, were captured, together with the said seal, which was delivered to Bruce, but he restored the signet to Edward on condition it should not again be used. The King of England thereby caused a new one to be made, and, to distinguish it from the other, entitled it his privy seal.[8]

It has been stated that Sir John Menteith, who betrayed Wallace, was liberated from prison on condition, his sons-in-law, influential men, being surety, that in the event of a battle he should fight in the front ranks of the Scottish king. This duty Menteith performed at Bannockburn so well and so bravely, that by his prowess, he not only procured pardon for his previous base behaviour, but received from Bruce a bountiful reward for his service, and continued a faithful subject to the end of his life.

King Robert, when a reasonable time had elapsed, gave orders that the bodies of the lords and nobility of England who were slain, so far as they could be recognised, should be honourably consigned to holy ground. This might be difficult, as both rich and poor, the former especially so, would be stripped and left almost naked on the field. Besides, the alteration of the features by violent death, might render it almost impossible to ascertain several of the men of note who had fallen.

The king also commanded that large pits should be dug on the field, wherein the scattered heaps of common people who had fallen

---

7. *i.e.* Was set at liberty free of ransom.
8. Bruce was more generous than Edward I., who placed the fragments of the great seal of Scotland in the Treasury of England.—Kerr, vol i.

might be decently interred.[9]

The king made the towers of Stirling Castle his place of residence for a time, and, having learned that the Earl of Hereford with his chief followers had taken refuge in Bothwell Castle, he dispatched his brother Edward with a sufficient force to that fortress, and after a short siege, the captain. Sir Walter Gilbertson, capitulated, agreeing to surrender Hereford with the other warriors into the hands of the king. The earl was accordingly sent to Bruce, who received him with respect and courtesy. By arrangement he was permitted to go to England without ransom, but in exchange for him, Elizabeth, the Queen of Bruce, daughter to the Earl of Ulster, Christian, the sister of Bruce, and Marjory the king's daughter,[10] Robert Wisheart, Bishop of Glasgow, who was blind,[11] and the youthful Earl of Mar, nephew to the king, were set free,[12] and returned to their own country.

The English, it would appear, had slight value by way of barter, for about the 20th November following, John de Segrave, an English baron who had been captured, was exchanged for five Scottish prisoners, David de Lindesay, Andrew Moray, Thomas de Morrain, Reginald de Lindesay, and Alexander, his brother.

---

9. None of these pits have yet been discovered. There are clumps of trees growing in lowish moist places over the field where it is supposed cottages once stood, and these appeared to the author as likely spots of sepulture. Still one or more of these depositories of mortality may yet be found. The skeleton of Robert Bruce in the church of Dunfermline was almost entire, when discovered in 1818; and south-west of Brankston, Andrew Rankin of that village, about 1820, cut a drain three and a half feet deep over a large pit of the bones of many of the heroes who fell at Flodden.

10. Marjory had been given in charge to Henry Percy, and she and Walter de Morrene were kept in the castle of Newcastle-upon-Tyne.—*Chron. de Lan.*, Note; *Foedera*, vol. ii.

11. Robert Wisheart, Bishop of Glasgow in 1306, held the castle of Coupar in Fife against the English. He was made prisoner there, arrayed in armour, and in that uncanonical garb was conducted to the castle of Nottingham.—*Hailes*, vol. ii.

12. The young Earl of Mar, nephew to the first wife of Robert Bruce, was imprisoned in 1306, but not chained on account of his tender years.—*Foedera*, vol. ii.; *Hailes*, vol. ii.

CHAPTER 13

Beneficial Results of the Battle

We cannot overestimate the value of Bannockburn to us a people. Had we been subdued never would we have mixed kindly in union with England. We should have been like Ireland, full of heart-burnings, jealousies, reluctance, hatred, strife, misery. Bannockburn stamped and sealed us as a people with a national history. After that we could well afford to be magnanimous, generous, and friendly in every arrangement with the great sister nation whom we had so triumphantly repelled. A broad calm of conscious dignity, a liberal national atmosphere, thus settled for ever around the glad head of Scotland.—Thomas Aird.

Among the lower ranks of the English who were unable to escape was Robert Baston, the Carmelite friar,[1] already mentioned. On being taken, and the aim of his mission told to King Robert Bruce, the churchman was desired to sing to another tune, with which he complied; and the result of his poetic ability is a Latin composition on the battle, consisting chiefly of rhyming hexameters. The piece is preserved by Bower in his continuation of Fordun's *Scotichronicon*.

All that the king and the English host had brought with them—beautiful horses, flocks of cattle, provisions of corn and wine in abundance, sumptuous clothing from the royal wardrobe and other sources, gay pavilions, splendid armour for the nobles and knights, vessels and utensils of silver and gold of vast value and exquisite workmanship, with the money chests and coin for the payment of the army, all fell into the hands of the Scots.[2] Cows, pigs, and poultry, with waggons,

1. From the vow made by King Edward during his flight to build a house for the White friars, he seems to have been very partial to that fraternity.

2. O day of vengeance and of misfortune! day of disgrace and perdition! unworthy to be included in the circle of the year, which

horses, and baggage of every description, must have extended almost from Foot o' Green on towards Falkirk. The loss to England amounted, we are told, to two hundred thousand pounds, the value of which, according to Tytler, may be estimated at about three millions of our present money.[3] Besides this, the ransoms paid by prisoners for their freedom would realise a very large sum, which is computed almost to equal the value of the plunder secured on the battlefield and in the English camp.[4] Bruce dealt out the spoil most liberally to his faithful subjects, and so very equitably, that all expressed themselves satisfied; indeed the whole Scottish army was enriched by the victory.[5] He also rewarded many of the nobles, who had done him good service, with possessions of a more permanent nature than money, and among the number Robert Fleming got the lands of Cumbernauld.[6]

Mention has been made of the two knights of Brabant, who were expelled from the English army on the night before the battle, and a reward set upon their heads by the King of England. They had been received by Bruce, and when he had leisure he bestowed on these men riches from the spoil gathered on the field, with which, on returning to their own land, they built a goodly house at Antwerp, calling it 'Scotland,' and causing a picture of Bruce, with the Scottish arms, to be set up thereon. The house afforded accommodation to Scotsmen from that time down, towards the close of the sixteenth century.

The articles used in besieging towns and demolishing castles, which the English had also brought with them, were carefully pre-

---

tarnished the fame of England, and enriched the Scots with the plunder of the precious stuffs of our nation to the extent of two hundred thousand pounds! Alas! of how many noble barons, and accomplished knights, and high-spirited young soldiers—of what a store of excellent arms, and golden vessels and costly vestments, did one short and miserable day deprive us?—*Mon. Malms.*, Tytler's Trans., vol. i.

3. The inquisitive reader may test the accuracy of this statement by the following extract:—'In the viii yere of the kyng (1314) was a Parlement at London, where was a gret ordinauns to chepe vitaile, and it avayled not. It was ordeyned that a oxe fed with gresse schuld be seld for xvis,; a fatte oxe for xxiiiis.; a fatte cow for xiis.; a good swyn, to yere old, for xld.; a shep withouten wolle, for xiiiid; a fatte schep with wolle, xxd. . . . . a capon, iid.; a henne, id.; iiii dowes, id., and if ony man seld ony othir pris, the vitail be forfete to the kyng.—*Capgrave.*

4. They got little lesse monie and riches by ransoming of prisoners taken at this battell, than of spoile gotten in the fight, campe, and field.—*Hollinshed.*

5. The spoile was so great of gold, silver, and other jewels gotten in the field, that the whole number of the Scotish armie was made rich thereby.—*Hollinshed.*

6. Robert Fleming, for his faithful service, gat the landis of Cummernald.—*Bellenden*, vol. ii.

served by the king, that they might be employed either against their former possessors, or other enemies of Scotland.[7] Probably they were used shortly afterwards in throwing down the fortifications of Stirling Castle, for when the king had arranged all matters relating to the overthrow of the English, he caused the walls and towers of that stronghold to be levelled with the ground. But out of all the property which the English left behind them, the rich stuffs and clothing were destined to be preserved for the greatest number of years. They were bestowed with other spoil to the cathedrals, the abbeys, and monasteries throughout the kingdom, as a thank-offering to God for the complete success with which the efforts of Bruce and his patriots had been crowned, in the deliverance from thraldom of their native land. Fashioned into altar-cloths, copes, and other sacred vestments, they would be regarded for several generations as relics of the memorable day on which Scotland achieved her freedom at Bannockburn.[8]

Allusion has been made to the servants of the English and the camp followers. We may suppose that these and the numbers who intended to reside in Scotland, expecting it to be conquered, would be subject to great suffering, for they were left in the midst of enemies who were stirred up to revenge by the wrongs they had endured from England, and were perhaps too ready, when the day of retribution came, to inflict punishment upon the innocent for the actions of the guilty. Some, probably, were wantonly butchered, others might suffer death in various ways, while many would find their position hard enough to undergo. Numbers might get away, for, if their clothing was scanty, and they had health, the season was favourable for escape. Even of those who endured much, compassion in calmer hours might follow, and it may be presumed that many a homely Scottish matron, touched with the wretchedness of the poor outcasts, afforded them relief in their wanderings, gave them food to eat, and administered to their wants, in the faith that they were acting up to the better and nobler impulses of our nature, and accordingly would not be without reward.

The result of the battle being remarkable considering the disparity

---

7. Bower, in his continuation of *Scotichronicon*, describing the result of the Battle of Bannockburn, says 'all the English provisions fell into the hands of the Scots, with their petraries and shovels, rafters and mangonels, ladders and engines, pavilions and bell-tents, slings and bombards, and other machines of war.'—*Meyrick*, vol i.
8. The goldin and silkin claithis, of quhilkis King Edwardis palyonis war maid, war distribut amang the abbays of Scotland, to be vestamentis and frontallis to thair altaris; of quhilkis mony yit reraanis to our days.—*Bellenden*, vol. ii.

of numbers on each side, the Church was not slow in imputing the good fortune of Scotland to the immediate interposition of heaven. On the evening before the battle, says the Canon of Aberdeen, there came to the Abbey of Glastonbury, which at that time, like other religious houses, was open to receive strangers, two men in singular clothing, who asked to be accommodated for the night. The abbot received them kindly, gave them good cheer, and, in the course of conversation, made inquiry who they were, and towards what quarter they were bound. They observed that, being servants of God, they were on the way to assist the Scots at Bannockburn. Next morning the chamberlain found they were gone before the gates were open, and the beds appointed for them were in the same condition as they had been left on the evening before. It was thereby believed these had been spiritual messengers sent from on high to succour the Scots in their righteous efforts against the unjust tyranny of England.

Likewise, from the same authority, we learn that on the same day the battle was fought, a knight, in bright shining armour, intimated to the inhabitants of Aberdeen how the Scottish Army had gained a glorious victory over their enemies of England. Soon afterwards this warrior, mounted on horseback, was seen to pass over Pentland Firth. He was believed by the people to be Saint Magnus, Prince of Orkney, and thereby King Robert endowed the church of Orkney with five pounds annually, out of the customs of Aberdeen to purchase bread, wine, and wax for the use of the abbey.

We are unable, even at this late period, to calculate the benefit which flowed to Scotland by the brave men, the most able and powerful of her whole people, who, under the direction of the greatest of her kings, fought and nobly accomplished the consummation of her liberties on this battlefield. Like the Greeks, fully aware of right and wrong, and aroused by their own heroic valour, these sons of freedom conquered here, and, though centuries since have come and gone, the event forms a sure step in the progress of civilisation, indicating that despotism must be subdued, and universal brotherhood be ultimately established over the whole globe. It follows that great men who have conferred renown on a country by which the people therein are elevated in the scale of humanity, have a memory green and flourishing, which survives age after age, as if they were still near, and had been known to us as intimate friends.

Wallace and Bruce, Randolph and Douglas, cannot die, for we remain their debtors, and, by venerating their names, we ever hold them in grateful remembrance. To us, accordingly, it is a gratification highly intellectual to visit and walk over land once trode by heroes; and when we stand on the very spot whereon they performed the principal triumph of their lives, we feel it is man alone that can invest a place with glory, and consecrate it by his noble actions, so that all must regard it as hallowed ground. The soil, therefore, of that battle-field, though cultivated and divided into sections by walls or hedgerows, is sacred, and must ever remain so to the latest period of time. Thus, to every Scotsman who feels proud of his country, no locality in Europe can possibly have the power to operate more suggestively on his thoughts, or inspire him with more grateful adoration to the Great Being who orders all things for good, than the solitary field of Bannockburn.

Concluding Remarks

We have not only heard it said, but a minor historian, (Thomas Keightley), has asked, 'what was the real gain to Scotland from Bannockburn, and would it not have been as well, since the whole island was to be ruled by one sceptre, if the union had taken place then as three centuries later?' We know the laws of the Plantagenets were equitable and beneficial, but had the arms of England gained the ascendancy at Bannockburn, the Scots under the one sceptre must have been considered and dealt with as a conquered people. Instead of this, when James the First came to occupy the English throne, the equality of both kingdoms had for many generations been established; and though Scotland was not so wealthy as the sister land, her sons were not behind their southern neighbours in arts, arms, and the other ennobling qualities which reflect honour on any country. Hence, when Scotland was united to England, the Scots, to their honour be it recorded, experienced neither abasement nor elevation by the change, whereas, had they in 1314 been subdued, their position from that date had been of the most abject description.

All ancient records, including portions of the Historical Books of the Old Testament, the works of Herodotus, Thucydides, the accounts of the Roman Empire, and that of England even down to the Middle Ages, show that the shedding of human blood by the baser passions of man, by warfare and other unhallowed designs throughout the world, made it resemble a den of wild beasts. Some cessation might occasionally be made in wholesale slaughter, yet it must be admitted that the weaker and undefended portions of humanity, including both sexes, were, from the upper ranks, subject at all times to oppression, privation, and death. A gleam of improvement was thrown over this sombre prospect by the institution of chivalry and its ameliorating influences, still it only resembled the sunshine of a wintry day flickering on the surface of frost and snow. Safety from outward assault there was none, unless it were possible that a person of undoubted prowess could remain isolated from society, and by means of rock, wall, and his own weapons and skill, defend himself against all aggression.

If, therefore, we keep in view the increasing power of England subsequent to 1314, and the probable inability of Scotland ever again to take the field with any chance of success in recovering her independence, no worse evil could have befallen the latter country than to be vanquished at Bannockburn. England proved by her hostility against the Scots at the time what treatment they might expect from their lordly conquerors. It is not the province of the historian to conceive, Dante-like, the perilous condition of the people of the northern land thus deprived of their honour, yet we may affirm it would be one of great severity.

Deprived of all that sweetens existence, humiliated, broken in heart and spirit, without hope of relief, and considering what they had to endure, death to the sufferers had often been welcome. Any Scotsman, under these circumstances, meeting with an Englishman, had been impressed with a sense of inferiority, and though indeed superior in some honourable qualities to the other, he and his descendants could only mourn over their state of degradation. Groanings, mutterings, and curses, would have arisen from every corner of Scotland; while the energy, the noble manliness, the strong desire for liberty, among her sons had been suppressed, and if possible stamped out by the domination of England. The hateful 24th of June, when it came annually round, had been to the Scots a day of wailing, sorrow, and despair, since it placed them in a condition of bondage, whence for ages they were unable to extricate themselves.

Thanks, however, be to Providence, Scotland maintained with the utmost fortitude her position against the foe, and nobly won the palm of victory. Nor did the sound of her exultation die away on the battlefield, or during the year of her fortunate struggle, but it was re-echoed for centuries, and will continue to be so over the length and breadth of her soil, telling her people to take heart and overcome all trial, for, like Paul, when confronted with the chief captain at Jerusalem, they can proudly say they were Free-born. Remembering this, with resolute and undaunted courage to maintain what is right and reject what is wrong, we trust that should peril ensue, like their invincible ancestors they will withstand to the death any attempt to impose on their liberty. Greece fought for this boon and conquered, but in a few generations her hard-won wreath of honour withered away. Scotland still preserves the priceless pearl in her diadem, and, though only a small province compared with the nations of the earth who are without that blessing, she exhibits a glorious lesson to the world that—

Who would be free themselves must strike the blow.

Defensive war only is reconcilable with justice, and when the rights of a community are threatened either by a tyrant or a foreign foe, it then becomes a sacred duty that they arm themselves and defy to the uttermost the insolent oppressor. Recent events prove it were well for all, if every despot was either destroyed like a wild beast, or immured in a cell and cut off from all connection with his fellow-men. It is on them he means to prey, their blood is to be shed, and their means wasted without hope of return on his account, while his aim is to hold them in bondage, and use them so that others also may be brought under his detestable sway. The peace of the world is evidently endangered when the sole command of any kingdom is vested in the power of a single individual such as king or emperor, though surrounded by counsellors; so that, for absolute security, a representative system of authority, founded on the widest possible basis, is preferable, whereby the will of the people, paramount at all times, can be brought to bear freely on every essential part of executive administration. Accordingly, we believe that in each enlightened community there is a tendency towards this form of government, and it seems to realise the truth of the poet's lines that the time will come

When man to man the warld o' er
Shall brothers be for a' that.'

We do therefore trust that better times will dawn on the world. Education, pursued till its fruit tell upon the multitude, will do much to open up a brighter prospect, for we have faith to believe that, by its influence, the prevalence of sober judgment, and consequent readiness to adjust human wrong, will cause devastating wars ultimately to cease. The inhabitants, however, of any land who aspire to be free must know how to estimate their own weight and power, must be able judiciously to regulate themselves, and, moreover, must be true and just men, otherwise liberty would be license to evil, and they would abuse the high privileges they seek to obtain. It is only by the regular exercise of self-control, and practice of the Christian virtues, whereby '*on earth peace, goodwill toward men*' are secured, that the people of any country can rise to greatness, or share to the full in the blessings that are enjoyed in a free state. With them the love of their own soil warms into patriotism, and thus, actuated by the finer feelings of our nature, the humble peasant, on contrasting his northern solitudes with the rich exuberance of the sunny south, may joyfully exclaim with Leyden—

> *Land of my fathers! though no mangrove here*
> *O'er thy blue streams her flexile branches rear,*
> *Nor scaly palm her finger'd scions shoot,*
> *Nor luscious guava wave her yellow fruit,*
> *Nor golden apples glimmer from the tree—*
> *Land of dark heaths and mountains! thou art free.'*

Appendix

NOTE A
Halbert's Bog and Milton Bog.

The author examined these bogs or marshes in the summer of 1830, and saw them both at that time covered and glistening with water, while the borders of each were fringed all round with thriving reeds and sedges. From the road at the bottom of Brock's-brae, Halbert's Bog extended up to a point in a direct line between New Park farmhouse and St. Ninians, while Milton Bog stretched down to where the bridge is erected on the turnpike road, south of the Whins of Milton. Both these swamps were drained by the respective proprietors in the summer of 1842, and the land now is excellent either for the plough or pasturage.

Originally they seem to have formed one sheet of water, but a passage in the centre, which was probably narrowest, having been made for the old road leading from Stirling to Kilsyth, the soil washed down by rain from the bank of Brock's-brae, which led up to the Bore-stone, divided at length the one lake into two. If any aquatic plants grew at the bottom of these large pools, they had above five hundred years, calculating from the time of Bruce, for growth and decay; and even if no such roots did grow there, from the natural deposit of ages, the depth of water must have decreased every century. It is not improbable that the hollow may have been used as a reservoir to supply the mills below with water, as the name of Caldam Hill would indicate, and Milton itself might possibly derive its designation from the said mills.

NOTE B
The Bore-stone.

The current tradition connected with the Bore-stone is, that in its hollow the staff of the royal banner of Scotland stood at the time of the Battle of Bannockburn. Nimmo, in his *History of Stirlingshire*, observes the hole in it was round, about four inches in diameter, and the same in depth.

The author saw it in 1830, and the impression on his mind is that the stone might be about sixteen inches in diameter; its colour was blue, and the hole in its centre had been square, each side being about five inches in length and the same in depth, but the edges of the opening were rounded, having been chipped away on every side by a succession of visitors, who intended to preserve the fragments as memorials of the great victory.

This mode of destruction seems to have been continued till the relic-hunters were in the habit of going to a smith's shop at the bottom of the bank, the site of which is now levelled for a small-bowling-green, and asking the occupier for the loan of a hammer to break off a bit of the stone to take with them.

The process unfortunately was carried on till the stone was broken, and some of the neighbouring inhabitants took away pieces of it for sale. Intimation of this being conveyed to the proprietor of the neighbouring land, he had the spot built round with stone and lime in a square form, about two feet high, and covered over with strong iron grating, fixed into the stones. It will be well if any remains of the original block still occupy the place.

The author is inclined to award all due deference to tradition, but in former times it was unusual to fix standard staves in stone in an open field, save in a stationary camp, such as that at the Borough-moor of Edinburgh, where James the Fourth drew his forces together ere they marched southward to Flodden[1]

In the time of battle the standard, instead of being fixed, was invariably borne before its owner, but so defended that it could not possibly be taken by the enemy. That of the Bruce at Bannockburn might have its staff placed in the ground ere the struggle began, but it would be raised by man's might, and held aloft, near to Bruce, during the whole of the conflict. Besides, the Bore-stone is nearly half-a-mile from the point where the battle commenced, and its size and socket was far too small and shallow to support the staff of a large standard, streaming and fluttering in the summer breeze.

The author's impression is that the blue stone may have been the base of a small cross, but whether erected before or after 1314, he is unable to say. Crosses were set up on the sides of roads, both in Eng-

1. *The Battle of Flodden Field* by Robert Jones is also published by Leonaur.

land and Scotland, for various purposes. When the plague devastated a town, the people drew near to a cross, as a place where they could buy and sell without fear of infection.

At a funeral, when the way to the place of interment was long, if the bier was set down at any particular spot to afford rest for the mourners, a cross might be reared there, like that below the old churchyard of Ettleton, in Liddesdale, so that travellers in passing might pray for the soul of the departed. Again, in former times, a cross sometimes occupied high ground on the side of a highway almost within view of a cathedral, to mark the limit of sanctuary, such as Neville's Cross, near Durham.

For this purpose there were, in 1144, similar memorials set up near the church of Lesmahago, which David II. granted as a cell to that of Kelso, with this privilege, that—'whoso, for escaping peril of life or limb, flees to the said cell, or comes within the four crosses that stand around it; of reverence to God and St. Machutus, I (the king) grant him my firm peace.' (*Innes*). Also, it sometimes occurred that before a battle a cross might be reared where the people, about to be engaged, might supplicate the Almighty for success. Or, if we suppose one to have been placed in the Bore-stone after the Battle of Bannockburn was won, what could be more appropriate, on such an occasion, than that every true Scotsman who drew near, then and afterwards, should kneel before it, as the point commanded a full view of the battlefield, and thank God for the deliverance of his beloved country from bondage!

When the body of Robert Bruce was conveyed from Cardross to Dunfermline, had the mourners passed this way and rested the coffin here, it had been well to mark the spot with a memorial of this kind. The author has read of the procession in some work that he cannot now recollect, but he believes the route they followed was not in this direction.

Note C.
Lists of English who were slain and taken prisoners at and after the battle.

No. I.

Nomina occisorum in bello commisso apud Stryvelin,[1] per Scotos, anno 1314, regni regis Edwardi II. 14.   fo. 7.

Barones mortui.

Gilbertus de Clare, comes Gloucestriæ.
Robertus de Clifford.
Paganus Tybetot.
Willelmus Marescallus.
Ancelmus Mareschall.
Johannes de Mountfort.

Milites Baneretti mortui.

Henricus de Bowñ.
Johannes de la Ryver.
Edvardus de Maule.
Johannes Comyn.
Robertus de Heestlegh.
Edmundus Comyn.
Willelmus Deyncourt.
Egidius de Argenthem.
Johannes Lovell.
Edwardus de Hastings.
Robertus Butvyleyn.

Oliuerus de Potton.
Robertus de Lisle.
Jacobus de Totorald.
Hugo de Scalys.

Milites et Nobiles in armis mortui.

Johannes de Elfeld.
Johannes de Pembrug.
Robertus de Poldesford.
Thomas de Vfford.
Reginaldus de Harecourt.
Robertus de Applingden.
Thomas de Coudray.
Thomas de Sentleger.
Reginaldus de Ayleby.
Robertus de Bertram miles.
Johannes de Caure.
Milo de Stapleton cum duobus filijs suis.
Walterus de Hakelytelb.

Nomina Valencium nobilium Angliæ capti ibidem apud Stryvelyn, anno 1314, et incarcerati sub custodia Roberti le Bruse regis Scotiæ, anno regni Regis Edvardi II. 14.

Humfridus de Bohun, comes Herefordiæ.
Comes de Anuges.
Willelmus de Latimer.
Johannes Gyffard.
Mauricius de Barkele.
Thomas filius suus.
Ingelramus de Humfreville.

Marmaducus de Theynge.
Johannes de Wellington.
Johannes de Claueringe.
Rogerus Tyrell.
Johannes filius suus.
Robertus Maulay.
Henricus filius Hugonis.
Thomas de Gray.

---

[1] *i.e.*—Bannockburn.

Walterus Beauchamp.
Johannes de Willington.
Ricardus de Charons.
Robertus de Fremiñil.[1]
Robertus de Omfravyle.
Johannes de Segraue.
Gilbertus Peche.
Thomas de Ferrers.
Thomas Boutetourt.
Antonius de Lucy.
Bartholomæus de Aynesford.

Richardus Byron.
Walterus de Skydmore.
Johannes Matrevers.
Thomas Thorney.
Rogerus de Sancto Johannes.
Philippus de Courtnay vel
   Surteney.
Johannes Bluet.
Nicholaus Scot.
Hugo de Hepham.
Edvardus de Hendale.

No. II.

Scott supplies this list at the end of his notes to *The Lord of the Isles*, but several of the names are incorrectly given, and the following were carefully transcribed from a copy of the continuation of *Trivet's Annals*, in the British Museum :—

From NICHOLAI TRIVETI Annalium Continuatio.

Oxford, 1723.

LIST OF THE SLAIN.

BARONS AND KNIGHTS-BANNERETS

Gilberto de Clare, Com.
   Glocestriae.
Roberto de Clifford.
Pagano Typetot.
Willielmo le Mareshall.
Joanne Comyn.
Willielmo de Vescey.
Joanne de Monteforti.
Nicolao de Hastelegh.

Willielmo Danycourt.
Ægidis de Argenteym.
Edmundo Comyn.
Joanne Lovel (divite).
Edmundo de Hastynge.
Milone de Stapleton.
Simone Ward.
Roberto de Felton.
Michaele Poinynge.

Edmundo Mauleo.

KNIGHTS *Slain.*

Henrico de Boun.
Thoma de Ufford.
Joanne de Elsingfelde.
Joanne de Harecourt.

Waltero de Hakelut.
Philippo de Courtenay.
Hugone de Scales.
Radulpho de Beauchamp.

Joanne de Penbrigge, Militibus.

una cum XXXIII. alliis ordinis ejusdem.

PRISONERS.

BARONS AND BARONETS.

Capti quoque & detenti sunt ibidem per Scottos.

Dominus Henricus de Boun,
  Comes Herfordiae.
Comes de Anagos.
Dominus Joannes Giffard.
Willielmus de Latemer.
Mauricius de Bekelegh.
Ingermanus de Umfroynule.
Marmaducus de Tewge.
Joannes Wyletone.
Robertus de Maulee.
Henricus Filius Hugonis.

Thomas de Gray.
Walterus de Beauchamp.
Richardus de Charonis.
Joannes de Wevelmtoun.
Robertus de Nevil.
Joannes de Segrave.
Gilbertus Pecche.
Joannes de Clavering.
Antonius de Lusey.
Radulphus de Canrys.
Joannes de Evere, &

Andreas de Abrembyn.

KNIGHTS *Prisoners.*

BARONES & BANERETTI, MILITES

Insuper subscripti capti & detenti ibidem fuerunt; videlicet :

Dominus Thomas de Berkeleghe.
Filius Rogeri Tyrel.
Anselmus de Mareschal.
Ægidius de Beauchamp.
Joannes Cyfrewast.
Joannes Bluwet.
Joannes & Nicolaus de
  Keirgestone, fratres.
Willielmus Lovel.
Henricus de Wiletoun.
Baldewinus de Frevile.
Joannes de Clivedone.
                 (Clindon.)
Adomarus la Souche.

Rogerus Corbet.
Gilbertus de Boun.
Bartholomaeus de Enefeld.
Thomas de Ferrars.
Radulphus & Thomas Bute-
  trort.
Joannes de Merewode.
Joannes Manfe.
Thomas & Odo Lele, Ercedekene.
Robertus Beaupel, filius.
Joannes Mantravers.
          (Mautravers, filius.)
Willielmus & Willielmus
  Giffard.

Cum aliis xxxiv. ordinis militaris. Et est summa Baronum and Banerettorum una cum Comite Glocestriae ibidem interfectorum XLII. summa vero Comitum Baronum & Banerettorum ibidem captorum & in custodia Scottorum detentorum XXII., Militium quoque LXVIII., Clerici quoque & Scutiferi plures ibidem fuerunt occisi & capti. De quibus & Dominus Rogerus de Northburge, Gustos Domini Regis Targiae ab eo ibidem oblatae, una cum Dominus Rogero de Wikenfelde & Thoma de Switone, dicti domini Rogeri Clericis, pariter detinebantur ibidem: ob quod dominus Rex cite postea fieri fecit sigillum, volens illud Privatum Sigillum appellari, ad differentiam Targia sic ut praemittitur ablata. Et est summa totalis tam Comitum Baronum & Banerettorum quam Militum intersectorum & captorum seu detentorum ibidem, una cum tribus Clericis praenominatis, CLIV.

Memoirs of Scottish Warriors

BRUS OF ANNANDALE.

ARMS OF SCOTLAND.

Robert the First, King of Scotland.

The many incidents in the life of King Robert Bruce have been narrated most amply by Barbour in his poem of *The Bruce*, by Kerr in his life of our gallant king, and by Tytler in the first and second volumes of *The Lives of Scottish Worthies*. Our space is limited, and we can only glance over the great actions of that heroic man, recommending those who desire to know more of him to any or all of these works, wherein they will find nearly all that is known of his history.

Robert de Brus, the grandfather of our hero, married Isabel, daughter of Gilbert de Clare, Earl of Gloucester and Hereford. His mother was Isabel, second daughter of David, Earl of Huntingdon, younger brother to William, King of Scots, and succeeding to his father as Lord of Annandale, he, in 1292, was competitor for the crown of Scotland. Dying at Lochmaben in 1295, his son, Robert de Brus, succeeded him in the Lordship of Annandale, and, marrying Margaret, Countess of Carrick, he became earl of that district by right of his wife. Possessing other estates in England, chiefly in the counties of Durham and Yorkshire, he performed no active part in the affairs of Scotland, and at his death, in 1304, he left to his illustrious son, afterwards King of Scotland, the lands and castle of Lochmaben, together with his possessions in Ayrshire, and resigned also to him the Earldom of Carrick. The great founder of the liberties and independence of his country was born on the 11th July 1274, but whether in the castle of Turnberry, on the Ayrshire coast, or that of Lochmaben, in Dumfriesshire, we are uncertain.

Reared amid arms and warriors, he would soon acquire the use of weapons, and when his grandfather and Baliol competed for the crown of Scotland he would be about eighteen years of age. Our hero therefore, from policy, adhered to the interest of England, and in 1296, when Edward the First removed the coronation stone from Scone to Westminster, he made fealty to him at Berwick, and, when about thirty years of age, he received seisin from the English King of the Lordship of Annandale.

After John Baliol was compelled to resign the kingly office to which he had been appointed, his nephew, John Comyn, having sworn fealty to Edward, stood nearest in right of blood to the sceptre of Scotland, and possessing very large estates, he was supported by numerous followers. Robert Bruce, aware of the wretchedness of his native country, is reported to have said to Comyn, 'Support my title to the crown, and I will give you my estate; or give me your estate, and I will support your claim to the Scottish throne.' Comyn approved of the proposal, an indented document was drawn out thereon, sealed by both parties, and an oath of secrecy taken. It is observed, however, that for his own purpose he acquainted King Edward with the agreement, and Bruce, being at court, on receiving a hint from a friend of his danger, instantly departed for Scotland.

No sooner did he reach the castle of Lochmaben than he went to Dumfries, where Comyn resided, and appointing a meeting with him in the convent of the Minorites, they met before the high altar, when Bruce reproached him with his treachery. A quarrel ensuing, Bruce stabbed him with his dagger, and hastened out of the place. His attendants, learning what had occurred, completed the tragedy, and also killed Sir Robert Comyn, who in the scuffle attempted to defend his nephew. This occurred on the 10th February 1305-6.

Robert Bruce had now committed a deed which Edward of England would never pardon. Only two paths were before him: he had either to become a fugitive, or assert his right to the Scottish crown. Accepting as a brave man the latter alternative, he was not without patriotic friends, and in six weeks afterwards he was crowned, at Scone, King of Scotland. In the course of six years from that date he underwent every privation that one in his position could possibly endure, and, to his honour be it said, he neither abated 'heart nor hope' in the prosecution of his design. During that period, out of four of his brothers, three were captured and executed by order of the English king. His queen, a sister, and his daughter, were taken prisoners, and kept in close confinement in England. Yet bravely he surmounted every difficulty, and by his own perseverance, his prudence, and wisdom, his exertions were at last crowned with success on the glorious field of Bannockburn. At this time he would be in the fortieth year of his age.

From his own generous nature, and the ameliorating influence of chivalry which he witnessed in early life, and which, like the spirit of Christianity, brightened up the darker recesses of human existence, he practised all courtesy in dealing with the English after he had made Scotland free. Nor was he slow in following up any advantage he gained if it tended to the security of the land he governed, for, in order to induce England to listen to terms of lasting peace, he harassed that country by successive inroads, enriching thereby his own territory. Desirous also of being reconciled to the Roman See, for he had been greatly traduced to Pope John by the emissaries of England, he induced the nobility of Scotland, in 1320, to draw up a manifesto, which they addressed to the pontiff, stating in precise but most comprehensive terms the position in which they were placed, and observing that 'so long as a hundred Scotsmen were left alive they would never be subject to the dominion of England. It is not,' they continued, ' for glory, riches, or honour, that we fight, but for that liberty which no good man will consent to lose but with his life.'[1]

After a prosperous period of thirteen years, in the lapse of which Scotland rejoiced in all the benefits she had won, a treaty was at last secured with the sister country, whereby Edward the Third, on the 1st March 1327-8, gave up all claim whatever upon Scotland, and agreed

---

1. A facsimile of the original of this important Declaration is given in the *Acts of Parliament of Scotland,* fol. 1844, vol. i., illustrated with representations of the seals of the several noblemen. A translation is printed in the collection of tracts entitled *Miscellanea Scotica,* vol. iii. Another copy appears in the *Harleian Miscellany,* vol. i. 8vo ed., 12 vols., Lond. 1808

it 'should remain unto Robert King of Scots, and his heirs and successors, free, and divided from England, without any subjection or right of service.' Within a few months afterwards, David, Prince of Scotland, married Joanna, sister to the King of England, so that peace seemed to be secured between both kingdoms. But within two years afterwards, on the 7th June 1329, King Robert died at Cardross, aged fifty-five, in full possession and enjoyment of all that in advanced life tends to our comfort and satisfaction:—

Honour, love, obedience, troops of friends.'

His remains were interred in the choir, near the high altar, within the church of Dunfermline, and a costly marble tomb made at Paris was shortly afterwards erected over them.

Robert Bruce may, without fear of contradiction, be accounted the greatest monarch that ever occupied the Scottish throne. The talents he possessed by nature, either as a statesman or warrior, were whetted and brought to the keenest edge by the long series of privations he endured, till the time came when he was enabled to turn them to glorious account. Even when surrounded by the pomp of royalty, and executing his kingly duties with promptitude, prudence, and wisdom, he never overlooked the poor of his realm, and was kind and generous to all around him. There could be no finer or more gentle trait than he showed to the poor washerwoman overtaken by the pains of labour in Ireland, when he stayed on her account his whole army, as it was about to march to the north. Barbour describes the circumstance very beautifully.

The compiler has often revolved in his mind the personal appearance of Bruce, being desirous to ascertain whether his complexion was dark or fair, and his stature high or low. The following single sentence from *Historia Majoris Britanniae*, ed. Edin. 1740, p. 194, may afford pleasure to those interested in such an inquiry:—

Erat enim pulchro, decoro & vegete corpore, latis humeris, venusta facie, flava more borealium caesarie, caeruleis & micantibus oculis, ingenio promptus, & ad dicendum vernacula in lingua orator acer & omnibus pergratus.

We have no cause to doubt the accuracy of this description of the great Scottish king. The fair or yellow hair is indicative of the sanguine temperament, and we know that Bruce was remarkable for energy both of body and mind. His strength was also evinced in the numerous encounters he had with the English at and previous to the Battle of Bannockburn. His descendants, the Stewards, though lacking his moral and intellectual power, inherited, so far as we can discover, some traces of the features and complexion of their illustrious ancestor.

Of the physical proportions of Bruce we have proof, from his grave being discovered, 17th February 1818, and opened in the presence of the chief officers of Scotland on the 5th November in the following year. The marble tomb which had been placed over it was entirely gone, but the skeleton was laid bare. The shoulders had been strong and broad, and the whole length, from the sole of the foot to the top of the cranium, was five feet eleven inches, therefore he had been about six feet high. A cast was taken from the skull, which is still preserved. There were four or five teeth wanting in the upper jaw, with a considerable fracture of the same in front, which had evidently been caused by a blow received, it is thought, in one of the encounters to which he was exposed in early life.

Bruce married first, Isabella, daughter of Donald, tenth Earl of Mar, by whom he had a daughter Marjory, who, in 1315, married Walter, the Steward of Scotland, but she died in the following year, leaving a son, who was afterwards King Robert the Second; secondly, in 1302, Bruce took to wife Elizabeth, eldest daughter of Richard de Burgh,[2] second Earl of Ulster, in Ireland, by whom he had one son, who, on the death of his father, became King David the Second, but he died childless in the forty-seventh year of his age. King Robert had also, by the said Elizabeth, two daughters, Margaret and Matilda. The said Margaret married William, Earl of Sutherland, by whom she had two sons, John and William. John died at Lincoln in 1361, and William carried on the line of the Sutherland family, which, after the commencement of the present century, was represented by the Marchioness of Stafford, Countess of Sutherland in her own right. Matilda, the other daughter, married a private gentleman, who, according to Fordun, was named Thomas Isaac.—See Kerr, vol. ii.

Arms.—Paternal shield when Brus of Annandale—Or, a saltire and chief gules. On being crowned, Bruce assumed the arms of Scotland—Or, a lion rampant gules, armed and langued azure, within a double tressure, flowered and counter-flowered of the second.

---

2. Crawfurd calls her Mary, daughter of Ailmer de Burc.

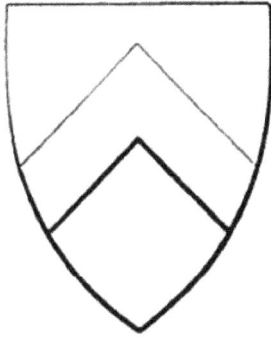

Sir Edward Bruce.

Sir Edward Bruce, brother to the king, was next to him in age, and performed an important part in the early history of Scotland. After the coronation of Bruce in 1306, he resigned to Sir Edward the Earldom of Carrick, with the title and dignity thereof, but, in default of heirs, the said earldom, with its honours, was to revert to the crown. Sir Edward was present at the enterprise against Perth soon afterwards, and on the failure of that attempt, he remained with his illustrious brother for a time, sharing in all his privations. But in 1308, when the fortune of his family seemed in the ascendant, he invaded Galloway, and with his usual energy attacked near Cree and defeated Sir Ingram de Umfreville and Sir John de Saint John, who commanded the inhabitants of that district for the King of England.

Afterwards Sir John de Saint John repaired to England, and collecting a large body of horsemen, he again advanced into Galloway, intending to circumvent and cut off Edward Bruce, but the latter, receiving accurate intelligence of his movements, arranged his troops, and bore down on the English so suddenly, that he put them to utter confusion, and on a second furious charge they were entirely overcome and put to flight. From the success of Sir Edward Bruce in this skirmish, he proceeded onward, everywhere reducing the people to obedience, and bringing them under the allegiance of his royal brother. About this time, it is probable that, being already the sixth Earl of Carrick, Sir Edward, for his gallant conduct, was made Lord of Galloway, which title he held till the time of his death.

He next comes prominently before us at the siege of Stirling Castle, where, his bravery being of slender avail, he agreed with the governor thereof, Sir Philip Mowbray, for a protracted surrender of the fortress.

Here he displayed great lack of prudence, and the result was the Battle of Bannockburn, in which, to his credit be it said, his bravery in war was most conspicuous. At length, when Scotland was rescued from thraldom, he went in pursuit of the Earl of Hereford, who, with a number of followers, had taken refuge in Bothwell Castle, and speedily forced them to surrender. In union with Sir James Douglas, he next led an army into England, penetrating as far as Richmondshire, and returned to his own country laden with spoil.

Nearly two years after the Battle of Bannockburn, the Irish chiefs of the province of Ulster were much dissatisfied with the English government of that country, and knowing how the Scots had successfully secured their national independence, they implored Robert Bruce to aid them in regaining their freedom, offering to accept his brother Edward as their king. Sir Edward Bruce, who had no scope for his martial energy in peace, probably considered it was no difficult matter to expel the English from that kingdom, and occupy the throne himself King Robert would appear to have assisted him in the design, for a great many of the nobility of Scotland accompanied Sir Edward in the expedition, which took place during May 1315. After undergoing various changes of fortune, and overcoming many obstacles, Sir Edward Bruce was crowned king of Ireland about a year after he effected a landing in that country. But his high position afforded him no relief from enemies at home and abroad, and he was slain at the Battle of Dundalk, in October 1318. In the previous year, a dispensation was granted by the pope, at Avignon, permitting him to marry Isabella, daughter to William, Earl of Ros, for they were within the third and fourth degrees of consanguinity, but he left no legitimate issue. Three natural sons—Robert, Alexander, and Thomas—survived him, who became successively Earls of Carrick.

Arms.—The old Earls of Carrick bore, Argent, a cheveron gules.

Thomas Randolph, Earl of Moray.

Thomas Randolph of Strathdon succeeded his father of the same name, who was Sheriff of Roxburgh in 1266. His mother was Lady Isabel Bruce, eldest sister to King Robert. His first appearance in public life was at the coronation of his uncle at Scone, in March 1306. Espousing the royal cause, he was taken prisoner by the English at Methven, and, through the intercession of Adam de Gordon, obtained mercy, being admitted to swear fealty to Edward the First. Again, in 1308, he was captured on Line Water, in Tweeddale, by James Douglas; and having in his defence spoken rudely to King Robert, he was ordered to close confinement; but being afterwards received into favour, he distinguished himself in 1312 by taking the castle of Edinburgh by escalade, he himself being the third assailant who mounted the ladder. It is supposed that soon after this time he obtained the charter of his honour, for, in the Parliament of 1315, he appears under the title of the Earl of Moray.

We have observed what trust was placed upon him by Robert Bruce previous to and during the Battle of Bannockburn, and how well he performed his duty on that eventful day. When the settlement of the crown of Scotland was made in 1315, it was enacted that should the heir be in minority, Thomas Randolph would be his or her guardian, and also Regent of the kingdom. After the death in Ireland of Edward Bruce, a second enactment was completed in 1318, whereby the heir to the crown, if under age, was to be placed under the tutorage of the Earl of Moray, who was also to be Guardian of Scotland, and failing him these offices were to devolve on Lord James Douglas. During 1319, Randolph, in conjunction with Sir James Douglas, commanded the army that invaded England, whereby victory was secured to the Scots near Boroughbridge, in Yorkshire. In the following year his name appears second on the list of those patriots who signed the remarkable letter to Pope John, wherein the independence of Scotland was so emphatically maintained, and which assisted afterwards in producing the happiest results.

In 1323 he went on an embassy to the pope, waited upon his Holiness at Avignon, and, according to Hailes, with the most consummate ability elicited from him an acknowledgment of the title of king to Robert Bruce. Two years afterwards he was sent ambassador to Charles le Bel, King of France, when he completed an alliance, offensive and defensive, between that kingdom and Scotland. About midsummer, in 1327, he and Douglas again led an army into the Bishopric of Durham, where they foiled the youthful Edward the Third, and returned with much booty into their own land.

When Robert Bruce died in 1329, the Earl of Moray became Regent of Scotland, and undertook the office of guardian to David the Second, discharging these duties with most exemplary fidelity, and, by his strict administration of justice, securing everywhere peace and prosperity to the people. But about three years afterwards, when the English were preparing to invade Scotland, the Regent Moray raised an army, and, though afflicted with severe pain from a confirmed stone disease, he exerted himself greatly, and died on the march, at Musselburgh, on the 20th July 1332. Some of our annalists observe he died of poison, administered by his chaplain, an English friar, through design of Edward the Third, but Lord Hailes contradicts the assertion. Barbour, however, puts upon record he was 'pusonit,' and Scott inclines to the opinion that the beautiful ballad of Lord Randal had its origin from that tradition.

Of the external appearance of Randolph, we learn from the pen of Barbour that he bore some resemblance to his uncle Robert Bruce.

Randolph, Earl of Moray, married Isabel, only daughter of Sir John Stewart of Bonkyl, by whom he got the barony of Garlics. He had two sons—Thomas, second Earl, and John, third Earl of Moray—both of whom died childless, and one daughter. Lady Agnes, who was married to Patrick, ninth Earl of Dunbar and March, who in her right became possessed of the earldom of Moray.

Arms.—Argent, three cushions pendent by the comers, within a double tressure, flowered and counter-flowered with *fleurs-de-lis* gules. The double tressure was added from Randolph being a son to the sister of King Robert Bruce.

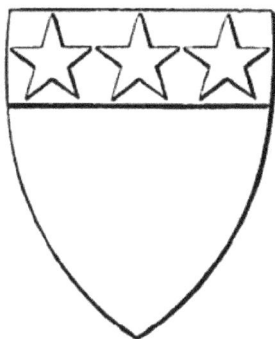

Sir James Douglas.

James Douglas was son to William Douglas, who, on the usurpation by Edward the First of the dominion of Scotland, withstood the tyrant, and being imprisoned, he died at York about 1302. His estates being forfeited, Edward had bestowed them on Lord Clifford; and James Douglas, a young man, being left almost destitute, went to France, and, probably by the assistance of friends, lived at Paris nearly three years. On the year after that of his father's decease, he returned to Scotland, and on presenting himself before William Lamberton, Bishop of St. Andrews, the good prelate received him with great kindness. The last time that Edward the First overran Scotland, he called together a meeting of the barons at Stirling, and Lamberton, having attended the summons, took with him the youthful Douglas. Watching an opportunity, he presented Douglas to the monarch as a squire who claimed to be admitted to his service, and asked that he would be pleased to restore him his inheritance. This was denied, and Douglas thereupon waited an opportunity whereby he might be enabled to lend his aid to the benefit of his country.

This was not long in presenting itself, for when Bruce had slain Comyn at Dumfries, and laid claim to the crown of Scotland, Douglas asked the bishop for leave to join his party. He obtained secret encouragement both by a horse which he was to secure against the will of Lamberton's servant, and by money, wherewith he was quietly supplied. He met Bruce at Erickstone, near the head of Clydesdale, who was journeying from Lochmaben to Glasgow, and the latter gave him open welcome. He was entrusted with the command of a party of men, and the Bruce soon found by his excellent qualities that he had secured an able supporter, who proved himself deserving of all confidence and honour. In the skirmishes and warfare which followed, Douglas repeatedly took from the English his paternal castle of Douglas, cutting off the garrison, and on the Borders he regained the forests of Ettrick and Jedburgh to the sway of Bruce.

Afterwards, on the water of Line, he took prisoners Stewart of Bonkyl and Thomas Randolph, who were in the service of England, and led them to the king, whom he assisted greatly in the invasion of Lorn, and in defeating the chief of that name, at the base of Cruachan Ben. His next great exploit was the capture of Roxburgh Castle, in 1312, when the English, who had possession of that fortress, were regaling themselves on the eve of Lent. At Bannockburn, he and the young Steward lent their aid in securing victory to the Scots, and after the battle he pursued the monarch of England, chasing him till the castle of Dunbar gave shelter to the fugitive king.

In 1316, when Bruce was assisting his brother Edward in his unfortunate attempt to maintain his position as king of Ireland, to Douglas was committed the charge of defending the eastern borders. The Earl of Arundel, being aware of the absence of Bruce, and knowing the prowess of Douglas, raised a large army to overpower him, but the latter, learning by spies of the approach of his enemy, drew him into an ambush in the valley of the Jed, and he was defeated. On this occasion Douglas, it is said, slew Thomas de Richmont with his own hand.[3] Many other daring and gallant actions he performed, the details of which our space forbids us to enumerate.

For several years Douglas assisted in leading the martial men of Scotland into England, and wasting and plundering the northern counties. On the last of these occasions, Edward the Third, then a stripling, opposed Douglas and Randolph, but he had no chance whatever in circumventing or beating back these tried and intrepid warriors. When at last Robert Bruce lay in expectation of death, he called Douglas and asked him to undertake the charge of carrying his heart to Palestine, that it might be interred in the Holy Sepulchre of Jerusalem, to which he readily agreed. Embalming the relic, and enclosing it in a silver case, he hung it by a chain around his neck,

---

3. Richmont, who commanded under the Earl of Arundel, entered the forest of Jedworth with ten thousand Englishmen, provided with axes to cut down the trees, and attack Sir James Douglas, to whom the defence of the march had been entrusted; but that cautious leader having constructed for himself and his followers a camp at Lintalee, a short distance above Jedburgh, issued thence, and giving battle to Richmont, killed him and routed his army.—*Whites Battle of Otterburn.*

and embarking with a goodly company at Berwick, he set sail, and on his track visited Alphonsus, the youthful king of Leon and Castile, who at that time was at war with Osmyn, the Moorish commander of Granada.

Our brave knight joined the Christians at once, and in a desperate encounter, detaching the casket containing the heart of Bruce, he threw it before him among the Moors, saying, 'Pass onward as thou wert wont, and Douglas will follow thee or die!'[4] In the violent onset he was slain, after which his mournful companions found his body, and the casket, which they conveyed home. The heart, by order of Randolph, was deposited in Melrose Abbey, and the bones of the hero were carefully entombed in the church at Douglas, among those of his forefathers.

According to Fordun, Sir James Douglas engaged seventy times in battle. Of these he was beaten in thirteen several encounters, and in the other fifty-seven he came off victorious. All his life he contrived, like Wallace, to defend his face from any scar; and this astonished the Spaniards when they saw him, and knew in what struggles he had been engaged. We have a striking picture of him in Barbour, who undoubtedly had the information from those who had seen him.

Sir James Douglas died unmarried, and had two natural sons, Sir William Douglas, called the 'The Knight of Liddesdale,' and Archibald, who was made prisoner at Halidon Hill in 1333. Sir James was succeeded in the Lordship of Douglas by his brother Hugh, and his youngest brother, Archibald Douglas, was made Lord of Galloway, and afterwards came to be Governor of Scotland.

Arms.—The old arms of the family, before Douglas became a surname, were. Argent, on a chief azure, three mullets of the field. But Sir James, on being commissioned by Bruce to carry his heart to Palestine, bore on his shield, Argent a man's heart gules, ensigned with an imperial crown proper, on a chief azure, three stars of the first.

---

4. This recalls to our thoughts all the desperate struggles he had encountered with Bruce, and is indeed highly poetical—more so indeed than Nelson's signal at the last of his battles:—*England expects every man to do his duty!*

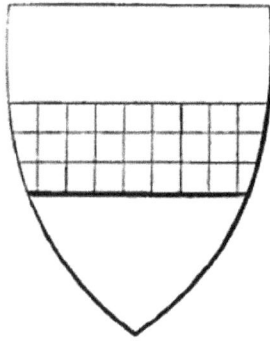

Walter, the High Steward of Scotland.

Walter, the High Steward of Scotland, was born in 1293, and succeeding his father James in 1309, he brought a gallant body of men to assist King Robert Bruce immediately before the Battle of Bannockburn. Along with his kinsman Sir James Douglas, as has been observed, he was appointed leader of one of the divisions of the Scottish army, and proved himself worthy of that honour. Towards the close of 1314, when the illustrious Scottish prisoners were to be returned from England, he was engaged to receive them on the borders, and, accordingly, he took under his charge Elizabeth, wife of King Robert, the king's daughter Marjory, his sister Christian, the young Earl of Mar, and Robert, Bishop of Glasgow. It is probable he thereby formed an attachment to the Princess Marjory, for they were married in the following year.

The union, however, was destined to be of short duration, for Lady Marjory died in 1316, leaving an only son, Robert, who afterwards became king. In that year, when Bruce passed over to Ireland to assist his brother Edward, king of that country, Walter the Steward and Sir James Douglas were appointed governors of Scotland. In 1318, when Berwick was recovered from the English, that town was committed to the charge of the Steward, who made every preparation for its safety, and in the following year he defended it against the King of England and a Royal Army, who were beaten off and compelled to abandon the siege. His name next appears among those of the patriotic nobles and barons of Scotland on the famous letter to Pope John, written in 1320.

Next year he acquired a grant of the lands of Eckford, in Roxburghshire, Methven in Perthshire, and Kellie in the county of Forfar, forfeited by Roger Mowbray; also, with the exception of the valley of Liddel, he got the lands of Nisbet, the baronies of Langnewton, Maxton, and Caverton in Roxburghshire, which had belonged to William Lord Soulis, the Seneschal of Scotland. Again, in 1322, the Steward, with Douglas and Randolph, by a forced march, attempted to surprise Edward the Second at Biland Abbey, in Yorkshire; but the king escaped with difficulty to York, and the pursuers, with five hundred horsemen, waited till evening at the gates of that city, that the English might come forth and give them battle. In this way, serving his king and country so long as he was able to perform such duty, he died on the 9th April 1326, aged 33 years.

Walter the Steward married, first, Alice, second daughter of Sir John Erskine, by whom he had one daughter. Secondly, in 1315, he led to the altar the Princess Marjory, whose son became High Steward, till he occupied the throne as Robert the Second. Thirdly, he married Isabel, sister of Sir John Graham of Abercorn, by whom he had a son and daughter.

Arms.—Or, a fesse cheque azure and argent.

King Edward the Second.

King Edward the Second was one of six brothers, sons of Edward the First, but three died in the lifetime of their father, and he, being the eldest living in 1307, ascended the throne in the twenty-third year of his age. Though of an affectionate and kindly disposition, he loved pleasure and worldly comfort, and was apt to leave state affairs to be transacted by his youthful favourites, rather than call together his nobility, and avail himself of their deliberation in arranging the more important matters of his kingdom. From this cause arose nearly all his misfortunes; and not alone did he endure the evils consequent on his inability, but the whole people of England, high and low, suffered less or more under his sway.

His first favourite was Piers de Gaveston, son to a gentleman of Guienne, They had been companions from boyhood, and the latter had considerable ability, was ready-witted, and in some tournaments he was enabled by his address to unhorse several Earls of England, Edward the First, perceiving the ascendency towards evil that Piers had gained over his son, caused him to be banished from the realm, and afterwards exacted from his son an oath that the dissolute youth should never be permitted to return to England. No sooner, however, had the father died than Gaveston was recalled, and loaded with honours and rewards, to the displeasure and enmity of the whole of the English nobility. Assaults and aggravation continued on both sides for the space of five years, till Gaveston, being chased as a fugitive, fell into the hands of the Earl of Warwick, who caused him to be beheaded on a hill at a short distance north from that county town. A wood now crowns the eminence, but the spot of execution is marked by an obelisk of a gray colour, which points upward from among the neighbouring trees.

On his other favourites, the Spensers, it is unnecessary here to enlarge. One of them accompanied him to Bannockburn; and here King Edward's lack of foresight and judgment has been plainly shown, previous to and at the battle, from the circumstance of causing his army to march towards Bruce as if he had been going to celebrate a marriage festival, instead of encountering the chances of war, and neither he nor his nobles provided any means of safety for the English forces in the event of a defeat. At the time of the battle, it may be observed, he was about thirty years of age.

Many serious quarrels arose between Edward and the chief men of his realm, which occasioned much bloodshed. This continued for the space of twelve years, for the nobility envied and hated Spenser, till at last they first brought destruction on the father of the object of their resentment, and afterwards upon himself. The wealth heaped on these favourites of royalty was enormous, the details of which are to be found in our historical authorities. Besides these evils, the Scots, under Bruce, Randolph, and Douglas, by frequent expeditions over the Border, caused much loss and suffering to the inhabitants of the northern counties. Rebellions were continued against the king, part of which he suppressed, but ultimately he was wounded in his tenderest feelings by one who ought to have proved through life his most faithful stay.

His queen, named Isabella, was a daughter of Philip le Bel, King of France. She was a beautiful, but an unprincipled woman. She bore him two sons and two daughters, and afterwards went to her relatives in France, where she plotted against him. An improper intimacy had sprung up between her and a rebel and exile, Roger Mortimer of Wigmore, so that when her lord and husband had become unpopular in England, she brought, with her paramour, a force over to this country, and by aid from the chief adherents of her designs, Edward was captured and imprisoned for a considerable period. He suffered much indignity, and by the wicked machinations of his enemies he was most cruelly put to death in Berkeley Castle, on the night of the 21st September 1327.

Arms.—The Royal shield bore. Gules, three leopards or lions passant guardant, in pale, or. The same insignia were borne by the king's father and grandfather, and he had them embroidered on his surcoat, and the caparisons of his horse. *Le Roy de Engletere, porte de goules, a iij lupars passauns de or.—Roll of Arms.*

Gilbert de Clare, Earl of Gloucester.

Gilbert de Clare was nephew to the king, his father of the same name having married Joan of Acre, daughter of Edward the First. He was born in 1290, so that, at the Battle of Bannockburn, he would be about twenty-four years of age.

After the death of his father, his mother Joan having married a squire, Ralph de Monthermer, who used the title of her first husband, yet her son Gilbert in the first year of Edward the Second, being in the wars of Scotland, is acknowledged by our historians as Earl of Gloucester, and though only in his eighteenth year, he had livery of his lands, the king having satisfaction that he was under age. Again, in the second year of the king's reign, he was captain-general of the nobles who were in his retinue, and in the year following he had several manors given him for life, in case he had no issue.

Next year, 1311, he was appointed Guardian of the whole realm of England, while the king was absent in Scotland. Moreover, before the battle of Bannockburn he was sent as one of the king's ambassadors to France to treat and conclude on certain articles of peace between both realms.

On his return he accompanied the king to Scotland; and being captain of the vanguard at the Battle of Bannockburn, he was slain, whereupon Bruce sent his body to King Edward at Berwick, to be interred where the latter should determine. Stow tells us his remains were buried at Tewksbury. He married Maude, daughter of John de Burgh, son of Richard Earl of Ulster, and left no children, since John his son died in his lifetime.

In expectation of issue, a considerable time was allowed to the said Maude, and, ultimately, his large inheritance was shared by his three sisters—Alianore, who married first, Hugh le Despencer, and secondly, William Lord Zouch of Mortimer; Margaret, wife first of Piers Gaveston, and secondly of Hugh de Audley; and Elizabeth, married first to John de Burgh, secondly to Theobald de Verdon, and thirdly to Roger D'Amorie.

The lady last mentioned, to her honour be it said, was the foundress of the College of Clare Hall in Cambridge,

Arms.—Or, three chevronels gules.
De or, a iij cheverons de goules.—Roll of Arms.

A drawing of this shield, whence the cut is designed, was kindly procured by the engraver, Mr. John Cleghorn, from a Roll of Arms of the English nobility who were present at a tournament held at Stepney, 28th February 1308, in Cole's MSS. vol. 47, p. 145, deposited in the British Museum.

Sir Giles d'Argentine was a hero of romance in real life.—HAILES.

Sir Giles de Argentine.

This warrior belonged to a family remarkable for bravery, who possessed lands in the counties of Cambridge, Norfolk, Suffolk, and Hertford. In 1193 Reginald de Argentine was sheriff for the counties of Cambridge and Huntington, and, four years afterward, entered into the like office for the counties of Essex and Hertford. Again, his son in 1223 was sheriff for the counties of Essex and Hertford, and was made Governor of Hertford Castle, Also, he became sheriff for the counties of Cambridge and Huntington, and in 1226 was one of the stewards for the king's household. This noble knight, of great prowess, went in 1229 on a pilgrimage to the Holy Land, but departed this life in 1246. Another of the family of the same name, being a Knight Templar, was standard-bearer of the Christian army; and in a great battle in 1237 against the Turks, near Antioch, in Palestine, he bore the banner till his legs and arms were both broken, and there he was slain.

Sir Giles de Argentine, another knight of great valour, and son to him who died in 1246, was constituted Governor of Windsor Castle in 1263. Joining, however, the rebellious barons after the battle of Lewes, in company with his son, he was elected one of nine counsellors to assume the government of the realm. But the insurrection being suppressed at the battle of Evesham, his lands were sequestrated. At his death, which occurred in 1282, he was seised of a certain manor lying in Weldburne, also of the manor of Great Wymondeley, in the county of Cambridge, which he held by grand Sergeantie, *namely*, 'to serve the king on the day of his coronation with a silver cup.' His son and heir, Reginald, was under age, but soon after his father's death, doing homage, he had livery of his lands in the counties of Cambridge, Norfolk, Suffolk, and Hertford. He was summoned as a baron to Parliament in 1297, but, dying in 1307, he was succeeded by John de Argentine, the second baron, who died about 1318.

The manor of Wimley or Wymondeley is said to have come into possession of the Argentines by marriage with the heiress of Fitz Tees, who was descended from David de Argentine, a Norman who came over with William the Conqueror. The male line ceased with John de Argentine, the fifth baron, and the manor was carried by his only daughter into the house of Allington, on her marriage with William Allington, an ancestor of the family. Of this line came the subject of our notice. Sir Giles de Argentine, but in what degree he stood we are uncertain. He was well known to Bruce in the court of England before 1306, and our archives afford us a glance into the military prowess of the man at the tournament already mentioned, which was held at Stepney, in which he attained, in the struggle for skill and strength, among the nobility of England the chief post of renown. In pursuit of the honourable profession of arms, he seems to have gone abroad, and in the wars of Palestine he encountered the Saracens on three several occasions, when in each conflict he slew two of their chief warriors.

He also entered the service of Henry VII. of Luxenburgh, Emperor of Germany, and following the brief but brilliant career of that illustrious individual, he acquired such fame as to be accounted one of the bravest warriors of his time. In common estimation the said Emperor Henry occupied the highest point of honour, Robert, King of Scotland, the second, and De Argentine maintained the third place. In 1313 he would appear to have returned to England, and from his acknowledged merit was appointed to remain by the side of King Edward on the field of Bannockburn. All our historians agree in extolling his bravery, and his loss was everywhere lamented. Bruce, from the intimacy which once subsisted between them, took especial care of his body, causing it to be buried in St. Patrick's Church, near Edinburgh.—*Bellenden, Hailes, Kerr*, etc.

Arms.—The bearings of De Argentine, as we learn from the Roll of Arms already alluded to in Cole's MSS,, were, Gules, three covered cups between nine crosses crosslet argent.

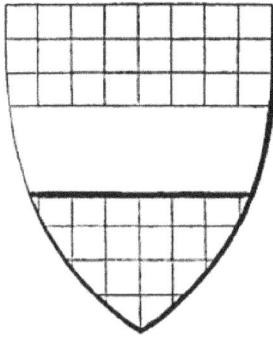

Robert Clifford.

Robert de Clifford, a noted warrior in the time of Edward the First, was born about Easter in 1274. When near his thirteenth year he succeeded his grandfather in his baronial honours. Dugdale says he was at the Battle of Dunbar in 1296. During the year following, in May, he was summoned to attend the king with horse and arms in an expedition beyond sea, and afterwards he was sent from Carlisle with an hundred men-at-arms and twenty thousand foot, to plunder the Scots, which he accomplished; and, after great slaughter, he returned to England with much booty. Forthwith he was appointed Justice of all the king's forests beyond Trent, and on the following year he was made Governor of Nottingham Castle. Again, in 1298-9, being constituted King's Lieutenant and Captain-General in the Counties of Cumberland, Westmorland, and Lancaster, and over Annandale and the Marches of Scotland, he was joined in commission with the Bishop of Durham and others to consider how the castles in England could be garrisoned, and how the Marches might be defended. Soon after, he was summoned to the Scottish wars, and received his first writ to Parliament at the close of 1299.

Thus, in his twenty-fifth year, he was honoured with his sovereign's confidence, and was present with him, in 1300, at the siege of Carlaverock Castle.[6] Here Clifford especially distinguished himself, for he served in the third squadron, and was led by the king in person. As a reward for his bravery he was appointed governor of the castle when

6. The French poem on this occasion, written it is supposed by Walter of Exeter, a Franciscan Friar, has excited great interest among heralds and historians. It was edited, as already stated, by Sir N. Harris Nicolas, and from the memoirs of the warriors in the volume the compiler has drawn much condensed information.

it surrendered, and his banner was placed on its battlements. On the year previous to the death of Edward the First, for his numerous services he had a grant of the borough of Hartlepool, and of the lands of Robert de Brus. He was also sent with Aymer de Valence against the said Robert, and, moreover, had a grant of the lands of Christopher de Seyton. At the death-bed of the king in 1307, he heard the monarch's orders to prevent the return of Gaveston to England. Under Edward the Second he was again Governor of Nottingham Castle, and was appointed Earl-Marshal of England. Soon after the wardenship of the Marches of Scotland devolved upon him, and he became governor of that kingdom.

Several additional grants of lands were also made to him in recompense of his services, and in 1313 he had an acquittance from the king for the jewels, horses, etc., which had belonged to Piers de Gaveston, for he adhered to the Earl of Lancaster against the royal favourite, and obtained pardon from the king for the active part he took in causing his death. He was regularly summoned to Parliament from 1299 to 1313, and fell, as has been stated, at Bannockburn, in the forty-first year of his age. His defeat by Randolph on the day previous to the battle may have led him to rush more unguardedly on the Scottish spears. His body is said to have been interred at Shap Abbey, in Westmoreland,

Clifford married Maude, daughter and ultimately co-heir of Thomas de Clare, Steward of Waltham Forest, son of Thomas, youngest son of Richard de Clare, Earl of Gloucester and Hertford. By her he had issue Roger, who, at fifteen years of age, succeeded him in the barony. Another son was Robert, from whom descended the baronial line of Clifford, which, in the time of Henry the Eighth, was raised to the Earldom of Cumberland. Some authorities say he had other two sons, John and Andrew, and a daughter, Idumea, the wife of Henry, Lord Clifford,

Arms.—Cheeky or, and azure, a fess gules. *Checkere de or e de azure, a una fesse de goules.—Roll of Arms.*

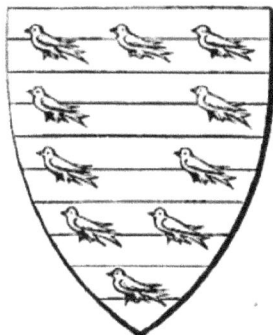

Aymer de Valence, Earl of Pembroke.

This distinguished man was born about 1280, being the third son of William de Valence, who was created Earl of Pembroke by his uterine brother King Henry the Third. About the sixteenth year of his age, he succeeded his father in his honours—two elder brothers having previously died without issue. He was tall in stature, and of a sallow complexion, whence Piers Gaveston bestowed on him the *sobriquet* of 'Joseph the Jew.' The earliest notice of him on record is, that in 1297 he was summoned to Parliament as a baron, though it is said he was entitled to the Earldom of Pembroke; yet that title was not bestowed on him in public records till 1307. It is, however, clear that from the decease of his father he ranked above all barons save Henry of Lancaster, who, being of royal blood, is mentioned next to earls.

About his eighteenth year he was sent by the king as an ambassador, to treat of a truce between England and France; and in the three following years he was in the Scottish wars, and accompanied the king in 1300 to the siege of Carlaverock. He was again in the wars of Scotland about 1302, and got permission to leave the realm on his own affairs. In 1305 the castles of Selkirk and Traquair, and the borough of Peebles, with other possessions in that kingdom, were granted to him to hold by the service of one knight's fee, and shortly afterward he was constituted Guardian of the Marches of Scotland towards Berwick, besides being entrusted with the sole command of the English forces which were levied against Bruce.

It has been mentioned that in the discharge of his office as leader of the English troops he established his headquarters at Perth, and after Bruce had been crowned, in attempting to reduce that town he was attacked suddenly by De Valence, and suffered a serious defeat. In the following year, however, Bruce met him by appointment, near Loudon Hill, and with a small body of spearmen, succeeded in vanquishing his squadrons of mounted horsemen so effectually that they fled in the utmost confusion to Bothwell. Again, De Valence was present at the death of King Edward the First, and, with other noblemen, received the monarch's injunctions to afford his son their support and counsel, so as to prevent the return of Gaveston to England.

Being summoned to Parliament by his proper title. Earl of Pembroke, he was present at the coronation of Edward the Second, and carried the youthful king's left boot, the spur belonging to it being borne by the Earl of Cornwall. In the same year, he was sent with Otho de Grandison and others to the pope on special business, and on the decease of his mother, by doing homage, he had livery of the lands she held in dower, and about 1310 he was found heir to the lands of his sister Agnes or Anne.

About this time he joined the Earl of Lancaster against Gaveston, and on banishment of that favourite, he was deputed, among others, to petition the king that he should be rendered incapable of holding any office.

Ultimately, Gaveston, with the king's consent, surrendered at Scarborough to Pembroke, who, on the way to Wallingford, leaving him in the custody of servants, he was taken by the Earl of Warwick and led to his doom. About 1313 Pembroke was sent on a mission to Rome, and obtained a grant of lands in London, comprising the New Temple. Early in the following year, being made Warden and Lieutenant of all Scotland, till the king should go thither, he was accordingly present at the Battle of Bannockburn, being stationed close by the king's bridle, and when defeat was inevitable Pembroke is said to have led him away. About 1316 he was commissioned to hold a parliament in the king's absence, and performed an active part therein. After this time he was sent to Rome on a mission to the Pontiff, but being captured on his return by a Burgundian named John de Moiller with his accomplices, he was sent to the emperor, who obliged him to pay twenty thousand pounds of silver, on the pretence that Moiller had served the King of England without being paid his wages.

About 1318 he was in the wars of Scotland, and we may suppose, on his journeys to and from the north, he regularly halted at Mitford Castle, in Northumberland, of which he was lord. Being appointed Governor of Rockingham Castle, he was constituted Guardian of the realm during the absence of the king, and held also the office of Custos of Scotland. In 1322 he fought on the king's side against Thomas of Lancaster, and was one of those who pronounced sentence of death against him at Pontefract, for which he was rewarded with the grant of several lands, chiefly in Northamptonshire.

During the following year he accompanied Isabell, Queen of England, to France, and when there he married his third wife, Mary, daughter of Guy de Chastillon, Count of St. Paul's, on which occasion he is reported to have lost his life at a tournament he gave in celebration of his nuptials, so that the bride was 'maid, wife, and widow,' in one day.

Dugdale, however, says he was murdered on the 23rd June 1324, by reason of the part he took in the death of the Earl of Lancaster. Nicolas, on the authority of a contemporary writer, which he quotes, considers it would rather appear he died of apoplexy. His body was brought to England and buried in Westminster Abbey, where his sumptuous monument is still seen.

Within the present century it had become much dilapidated, but by the means supplied by government, and the skill of the most able artists of the time, it was restored almost to its original splendour. It is depicted both by Blore and Stothard, whose works are of great value to the historian as well as to the antiquary. Aymer de Valence was thrice married, but left no issue; first, to Beatrix, daughter of Ralph de Noel, Constable of France; secondly, to a daughter of the Earl of Barre; and thirdly, to Mary, the lady above mentioned. His said widow came to possess large estates in several counties of England, and, to her renown be it added, she was not only a bountiful benefactress to many religious houses, but became the foundress of the college of Pembroke Hall in Cambridge, an act which, Nicolas observes, ' seldom fails to ensure immortality.'

Arms,—Barry, argent and azure, an orle of Martlets gules.
Burele de argent e de azure, od les merelos de goules.
Roll of Arms.

The Umfreville shield, taken from that on the effigy of an early Umfreville in Hexham Abbey church. Surtees, in his *History of Durham*, says the arms are, Gules, a cinquefoil within an orle of crosses patonce or.

Ingram de Umfreville.

Ingram de Umfreville, as Hodgson, the historian of Northumberland, relates, was, in all probability, brother to Gilbert de Umfreville, the first Earl of Angus, in right of his mother. He was a Scotch Baron, and comes prominently before the reader of Scottish history from 1291 to the period of the Battle of Bannockburn. It is likely that another of the same name, probably his son, figures before the public from the time of the Battle of Neville's Cross in 1346 down to the fiftieth year of Edward the Third, 1376.

It is accordingly the first Ingram of whom we desire to render some account. He appears, says Hodgson, 'as a luminary above the ordinary magnitude in the constellation of the eminent men of his time.' He was present at Norham, when the claims of the several candidates for the Scottish crown were arbitrated, and in the year following he witnessed John de Baliol do homage to the first Edward in the great hall of the castle in Newcastle-upon-Tjrne. In 1296 he surrendered the castle of Dumbarton to the King of England, and his two daughters, Eve and Isabella, were given up as hostages of his fidelity to that monarch. In the following year King Edward summoned him to march with his whole force against the rebel subjects of Scotland, but on this occasion we have some cause to suspect he was disobedient, and may have favoured the independence of that country.

In 1302, the Scots sent him to France to watch over the interest of their land in the negotiations which were about to take place. During the year afterwards, he wrote to John Comyn, Regent, and his party, a storming letter, telling how a peace had been settled between

England and France without including Scotland therein, and urging them to stand out boldly and maintain the rights of their own country. In 1305, however, he had again embraced the English interest, and subsequently Edward the Second took him into favour, making him a warden in Galloway, and one of the council of Robert de Clifford. In 1308 he was defeated by Edward Bruce in that district, and on his forces being cut off, he escaped with difficulty to Butel Castle. Barbour relates that about this time Umfreville caused a red bonnet set upon a spear to be borne about wherever he went, to indicate that he had attained the height of chivalric prowess and bearing.

By a writ directed by Edward the Second, in 1309, to the Sheriff of Northumberland, Ingram de Umfreville claimed twelve messuages, one hundred and twenty acres of land, eighty acres of meadow, three hundred acres of wood, and one thousand acres of pasture in Elsden, in Northumberland, as related and next of kin to Gilbert de Umfreville, then deceased. Shortly afterwards King Edward ordered his warden of Scotland to see that Umfreville was bountifully supplied for the good service rendered to his father and himself. He is styled baron in 1310, and empowered to take into the king's allegiance such Galwegians as had been opposed to him but wished to be received into the royal favour.

Afterwards he appears to have taken part with the Earl of Lancaster in accomplishing the death of Gaveston, for his name is in the list of those who received pardon for that occurrence. His reply to the King of England at Bannockburn, mentioned in the text, is the last notice we have of him, so far as the compiler has seen among the public records, in the early period of the fourteenth century.

We have no record either of his marriage or of what issue he left, but one of the same name, as has been observed, was known in public life for above fifty years after the Battle of Bannockburn.

Arms.—In the Roll of Arms of the reign of Henry the Third the Umfreville arms are—Or, a cinquefoil gules, within a bordure azure *semée* of horse-shoes or. Again, when Sir Gilbert of that name married Matilda, Countess of Angus, by whom he became Earl of Angus, his arms, according to Nisbet (vol. i.), were—Azure, a cinquefoil within an orle of eight cross crosslets or. The only notice I have seen of the arms of Sir Ingram de Umfreville is in *Documents of the History of Scotland, 1286 to 1306, selected and arranged by Joseph Stevenson, Esq.: Edinburgh,*

1870, 2 vols.' In vol. ii., we observe that, to a 'Promise' made by the Scottish Commissioners in France, dated Oct. 22, 1295, Umfreville's seal is attached 'by a cord of green silk. It is uninjured, and a very beautiful specimen of art.' The original is deposited in the Imperial archives at Paris, S. H. S. J. 457, No. 3.

www.ingramcontent.com/pod-product-compliance
Lightning Source LLC
Chambersburg PA
CBHW021055090426
42738CB00006B/344